THEATRE OF ANIMATION

CONTEMPORARY ADULT PUPPET PLAYS IN CONTEXT – 2

Contemporary Theatre Review
1999, Vol. 10, Part 1, pp. iii–iv
Reprints available directly from the publisher
Photocopying permitted by license only

Contents

Contemporary Theatre Review
1999, Vol. 10, Part 1, pp. 1–12
Reprints available directly from the publisher
Photocopying permitted by license only

Introduction

Puppet theatre consists of integrated design, movement and speech systems of equal importance. This collection concentrates on the latter – on text-driven puppet dramas and how the 'word', what is written for performance, integrates with the other art forms involved in the making of a work for performers using puppets in theatre (cf Appendix A: Puppet Theatre Questionnaire).

The collection aims to provide a representative selection of current puppet theatre texts written for live performance for an adult audience by interesting and experienced companies concerned with contemporary issues. (It does not include work written for T.V. or for film which would widen the scope beyond the bounds of a single issue.) It considers the definition of 'puppet' to be broadly 'any theatrical figure or object moved under human control' (Tillis, 1992). The wide field dictates a definite limitation of the area covered – the journal issue includes work from Europe, Britain, the USA and the former Colonies. It represents only a small number of puppet plays available, though there are relatively few texts in comparison to the number of theatre of animation pieces with little or no text being performed today.

Where necessary, the editor requested that contexts of 'scene', movement, additional visual and sound material were added in written form to become part of the published work.

As puppet theatre drama is best suited to certain genres, the selection includes: satire (Howard Barker's *All He Fears*; surrealism (Johanna Enckell's *Nuptial Nights*); absurdism and the bizarre (Dennis Silk's *The Head or Watch it, Kid!*); the grotesque (Doo Cot's *Odd if You Dare*); an adaptation, including the surreal and the grotesque for satiric ends (Handspring Puppet's *Faustus*).

The essay accompanying a text was mostly written by the company writer in response to the editor's devised questionnaire (cf Appendix A).

a) Devised Puppet Theatre Texts : The Image, the Puppet and the Text

Puppet theatre, like modern 'physical' theatre, is generally seen to take its main thrust from image, gesture and design rather than from the word. It is primarily a spectacle, with its roots in an oral tradition in which text is seen as secondary, often improvised and spontaneous, worked up by the puppeteer from a scenario, a storyboard or a series of random episodes, in the spirit of the anarchic and the carnivalesque. In this kind of puppet theatre, the manipulator's interchanges with the puppet-performer constantly varies i.e. the text is not necessarily 'fixed'. Only when the text needs to be reproduced is it written down. *Punch and Judy* is a good example of this kind of devised text with a long oral tradition. George Speaight points out that *Punch and Judy* has no author or story, no meaning and no moral. It is a series of unplanned encounters by the comic and anarchic figure of Punch, the hero (worn – if it is a one-man glove-puppet performance derived from the earlier baroque marionette versions – on the puppeteer's right hand, whereas those he defeats i.e. Judy, the Baby etc. are operated on the left hand). It is derived from the old puppet theatre shadowing of the travelling commedia dell'arte characters from Italy, and perhaps France, combined with England's indigenous clowning traditions. Gradually the situations and the characters in the performances became more 'fixed', though the text continued to be improvised by performers. The text – *The Tragical Comedy or Comical Tragedy of Punch and Judy*, first published by Septimus Prowett in 1828 with Cruikshank's illustrations, was adapted and edited at the time by John Collier, a student of English drama, who recalled the street performance of an old Italian, Piccini. He remembered it from his childhood, wrote it down and edited it. Many versions have followed (Speaight, 1990). Henryk Jurkowski argues that the authenticity of the text is debatable, but he acknowledges that most experts recognise it as fundamental and a point of departure for studying the text. Unlike Speaight, Jurkowski argues that Punch, who imagines the world is run for his needs alone, *is* cruel when his egoism is challenged, though Punch has our sympathy because he is so inventive and pragmatic in his ability to survive, and he mocks and anarchically defeats the despised social institutions. Whereas Speaight sees Punch as amoral and merely part of a series of knock-about encounters that 'happen', in which the character of the 'clown' commits murder as the quickest way of ending a scene, Jurkowski reasons that Punch exists to help the audience to a kind of freedom via his anarchy. (Jurkowski, 1991)

In the collection of recent puppet theatre texts in this issue, perhaps Doo Cot's *Odd if you Dare* comes closest to this kind of devised piece, though it is written in a postmodern form of a mixture of stylistics on several levels. The story of the violent death of an abused woman is devised from 'snippets' of stories or images gathered and pieced together from newspaper cuttings etc. However, the company depends first on 'visuals' – the two main puppet characters are like personalised life-size figurative paintings made by Nenagh Watson's collaborator, the painter Rachel Field, that have 'walked off the wall'. The audience wonders which is more important – the puppet or the live person/puppeteer manipulating it, and whom it resembles. The other puppet characters are more caricatured and stylised, mixed with threatening and grotesque or surreal objects made from scrap material that reflect the piece's preoccupation with violence and death. Once the sculptural image of the puppets has been formed, the dimension of music is provided by the composer Sylvia Hallet, as a source of emotion that matches the 'emotional being' of the puppets and the chosen 'gestures' they perform. Songs are an important part of the written text: they aim at being concrete and poetic. The final song was written to stand outside the rest of the text as a deliberate confirmation of life – of the human singers – in the face of the death of the female puppet characters. The rest of the text is then written and is deliberately cut-down and stylised in keeping with the postmodern mixing of styles. The text on tape is a random series of recorded voice elements mixed with suggestive and threatening sounds, together with the changing scraps of visual material that flicker across the backdrop on video.

b)   Written or 'Literary' Dramatic Puppet Theatre Texts: The Text as Point of Departure

There is a rich and varied repertoire which stretches far back in time, of literary theatre texts specifically written with puppets in mind. Puppet theatre has its own history and development that runs apart from but parallel to 'live' theatre. At particular moments in that history, puppet theatre has come to the fore and influenced the writing and production of 'real' theatre because it challenged the values inherent in its traditions and values. Foote, Kleist, Gordon-Craig and Kantor (though these initiators were often primarily directors rather than writers), wished to experiment with the actor as puppet rather than with the text. Other adult puppet theatre writers like Jarry, Strindberg, Maeterlinck, Lorca and Ghelderode, were experimentalists working on the fringe of 'live' theatre, intent on creating their own 'dream' worlds in the language of theatre, rather than on writing puppet plays of excellence. (cf 'Puppet Theatre – the Repertoire' at the end of this Introduction.)

In this collection, Howard Barker's *All He Fears* is a commission for the puppet theatre company Movingstage and specifically written for performance by marionettes. Artistic director Gren Middleton believes that 'the better the text the better the show.' (cf Middleton's article 'Why Promote Text-based Drama for Live Animation?' in this issue.) The writing of the play is down-to-earth but 'made strange' by a bizarreness in the language. Barker writes that he thought of the play primarily as a poem, ignoring the problems of staging it as a play (cf Barker's interview with Penny Francis in this issue.) The text keeps to a single mood – Boethius the philosopher's self-regarding mournfulness, full of comic and horrific perception of the meaning of his own wilful and self-determined downward spiral into the hell of his own madness. He does this despite humanity's initial gestures of kindness to him, because he prefers pain and suffering to enduring a world in which political conservatism and materialism dominate. Barker takes into account in the stage instructions, the movements and gestures of the puppets. These include a delightful giant Rat, a projection of Boethius' unconscious, and several puppet-characters who defy their stylised forms with their unexpected 'human' quirkiness. Barker creates a precise visual picture with the language, often deliberately separating gesture from word, though the two are united in spirit. The events or 'visuals' written into the piece are marvellous black-comedy – the 'in-terior' feelings given grotesque and fantastical exterior form. Boethius' madness, for example, is represented by red ribbons that spill out of his head and fall about him so he can touch them and so pass mournful comment on his own state of being.

Handspring Puppet's adaptation of the Faustus legend is based on Goethe's *Faust* and uses a modern translation by Robert David MacDonald with rap additions by the South African poet Lesego Rampolokeng. Adaptations are an ancient and popular form in puppet theatre writing and particularly suitable for the medium. This adaptation transfers Faustus' story to Africa in the colonialist 1920's, not only as an anti-war play, but as a modern and satiric reinterpretation of the legend – God is more or less ignored, Mephisto decides not to return to Hell with Faustus and instead, remains with him to play cards. The emperor who was once Faustus' domestic servant, declares a general amnesty saying: 'those who poisoned our streams will design our irrigation schemes.' 'Some find this deeply cynical, others recognise how close a parallel there is with our present government' (Basil Jones). The text is modern, deliberately light and mocking in tone, but the language retains a strong rhythmic formality in the verse pattern of rhyming couplets, sometimes developing into incantation and verse-song. The puppets were made first – deliberately rough-hewn – locating 'character' in references to research material on Africa of the 1920's. Then the animations were developed i.e. the tape of the moving images – rough charcoal drawings by the painter William Kentridge, together with extensively researched documents depicting Africa in the nineteenth and twentieth century that were projected behind the puppets being 'moved', as in Bunraku, by two 'guardians' apiece, in full view of the audience. Finally, the company matched the tape to fragments of the text and the puppets' movements, having edited the animation to give the best sense of shape and space to the piece, and allowing each scene to be driven by performance rather than by the speed of the tape. The skill of the performance of the text lay in the timing of the co-ordination of puppets, animation on screen and text. This was helped by the fact that most of the performers were trained actors who then worked as puppeteers. For the purpose of publication, each 'scene' and the 'contents on the screen' has been described. The drawings are witty 'translations' of the text into surreal imagery – a grapefruit becomes a land-mine; Gretchen, a nurse, looks down her microscope at the jewels that the wealthy colonialist soldier and explorer Faustus gives her and we see, on screen, her vision of the 'jewels' as insects on the stump of a severed arm.

Writing for Puppet Theatre versus Writing for Live Theatre

From the above descriptions of how puppet theatre performance changes the nature of a script, it becomes clear that writing a drama text for puppet theatre is very different from writing a 'live' theatre play.

Puppet-Actors Differ from Human Actors

The Swedish leader of puppet theatre, Michael Meschke, writes in his notes to his play 'Music from Sarajevo' (not included in this collection) that after 40 years of experience as a puppet theatre director and dramaturg, 'to work with puppets requires deep knowledge about the specific laws and aesthetics of puppets.' He is concerned that what little there has been written expressly for puppets is 'often based upon narrow concepts of that art, marked by moral standards of the last century or using puppets in a symbolic, literary sense, far from concrete understanding of the art.'

This approach is made clear in Johanna Enckell's essay 'Theatre of Actors and Theatre of Animation' accompanying her play *Nuptial Night*. She suggests that the writer must recognise the difference between the actor and the puppet-actor in order to write an effective puppet theatre piece. The 'live' actor learns to take into himself a 'character' via a complex and subtle process of assimilation that changes and grows. A puppet – manipulator on the other hand, deals with a cartoon representation of character that can only be projected by the 'manipulation' of the inanimate puppet. Henryk Jurkowski takes this difference further: he states that in puppet theatre the puppet is made to speak and move by the puppeteer who is quite separate from the puppet – the voice and movement come from outside the puppet. (Jurkowski, 1988) Also, the actor in puppet theatre may be both the puppet and the animator, and the source of the voice and movement may change through a performance, which does not happen in 'live' theatre.

Eric Bass, in his essay 'Notes on Puppetry as Theatrical Art' in this journal issue, writes that the texts he uses for puppets are 'created through dialogue between my idea of a particular puppet and my sense of what the puppet "wants" to do.' He might change the text to suit the puppet or vice versa. 'I try to remember that the puppet is a metaphor for some aspect of the text, or an embodiment for some image of the text.' In other words, he sees the puppet for which he writes as a metaphor.

Dennis Silk's intriguing essay 'The Marionette Theatre' influenced by Gertrude Stein's writing and aesthetics, includes both the performer and the watcher in the metaphor of a marionette or 'dismembered man – a thing and yet a man' – with a body composed of separate parts that must try and act together but which are uncontrollable. He sees the puppeteer as a boy playing in a 'toy-theatre' with a toy that comes apart in his hands. The puppeteer can imagine these parts as alive, and so makes new connections with them that are absurd and grotesque. (Hence the title of his piece *The Head or Watch it, Kid!*) A form of animism is at work – 'a man of parts' is Silk's pun on the image as the 'parts' take on a new life of their own both in the puppeteer's and the audience's imagination and memory – an uncontrollable, inventive and bizarre force. This releases the puppet's actions into a terrifying, cruel and surreal world where anything can happen. This puppet-figure or 'dismembered man' is also ourselves, a kind of puppet split between the two persona of the actor and the 'self' that helplessly watches the 'other' – a metaphor for man as a cruel and heartless automaton which is at the same time helpless – a puppet, trapped in his own 'woodenness'.

Edward Gordon-Craig's Uber-marionette

Early in his career, Craig was fascinated by puppet theatre and wrote his own plays for puppets, and so became interested in the idea of making 'live' actors more like puppets. His own puppet plays are rather lifeless and unworkable for performance. However, as the outstanding English director of his day and exponent of symbolist theatre, he was attracted to puppets because he saw in them a parallel to a means of completely controlling his actors on stage, thus allowing him to realize his director-centred vision of a play's performance. To Craig, the actor's very 'humanness', his emotions and self-consciousness was a flaw for the director. His ideal, therefore, was to be able to actually substitute the puppet for the actor onstage. In his essay 'The Actor and the Uber-marionette' (1907) he wrote: 'They (the actors) must create for themselves a new form of acting, consisting for the main part of symbolic gesture... The actor must go and in his place comes the inanimate figure – the Uber-marionette... the descendants of a great and noble family of Images.' In other words, the actor should model himself on the puppet, with its obedience and awareness of silence. He played down the importance of language and emphasised instead the language of the body in space. (Segel, 1995)

The Alienation Effect in Puppet-Character: The Influence of Japanese Bunraku

The great Russian puppet-master Sergei Obratzov, who wrote the texts for his puppet performances, points out in his autobiography *My Profession*, that the puppet theatre is the most allegorical of all the arts because the puppet is an 'allegory' in itself. The writer must realize that the character created on a puppet stage is felt by the actor as being outside himself – the actor becomes the director of his own role: he not only creates the puppet-behaviour, but observes the results i.e. Brecht's 'alienation' effect is brought into play in puppet theatre. This effect can be illustrated by the Japanese puppet theatre, Bunraku. In Bunraku, the voice comes from the special 'chanter' of the text, while the puppet is moved by three visible operators, two of them hooded, who do not speak, though the third, unhooded operator uses facial expression to mime each character's emotions, and all three drum their feet to add to the effect of the accompanying musician. The chanter, while 'singing', also expresses in movement each puppet's emotions. All these elements are of equal importance in performance and have influenced modern puppet theatre performances across Europe today. Jan Kott comments on Bunraku as 'evoking absolute illusion and its equally absolute destruction. Bunraku is simultaneously a theatre in which puppets act human drama – and a metatheatre whose protagonists are the manipulators operating the puppets, the narrator and the musician – a metatheatre, whose dramatic action consists in revealing the theatrical illusion.' (Tillis, 1992).

The effect this has on the audience is that the puppet is seen with a double vision – as being both 'alive' and an 'object' at the same time – the audience must supply the puppet with the 'consciousness' it lacks. This gives the puppet its special quality of mystery or 'grace'.

The Actor Centre-Stage in Modern Puppet Theatre/Theatre of Animation

Though 'pure' puppet theatre is still performed, a 'third genre' exists, situated between live and puppet drama, mixing the means of expression of both and giving a new metaphoric language to theatre (Jurkowski, 1979). It favours the actor over the puppet, but, as modern 'physical' theatre already tends to stylize the actor, this is not unexpected. *Perhaps this is the single most important new development in puppet theatre today – the actor has become more important on stage than the puppet.* Perhaps this highlights the need for a stronger more 'written' text. Not everyone involved in puppet theatre welcomes this new emphasis on animation rather than puppetry. There is an awareness that the ancient and complex art-form of puppet theatre is being sacrificed and that unless puppet theatre is used as the main art form, the trend will damage puppet theatre as a whole as the modern influence of animation has placed the actor, rather than the puppet, centre-stage.

How do these Conditions and Limitations Affect the Writing of a Puppet Theatre Piece?

Sergei Obratsov sets out a clear description of writing techniques for puppet theatre in his autobiography *My Profession* (Obratsov, 1957). Trained as an actor and a master puppeteer working at the turn of the century, his advice to writers of puppet texts still stands. It is interesting to note that Obratsov gives 'the word' priority i.e. he believes that the text plays a large part in creating the image of the puppet, but he insists that the writer must imagine the puppet on stage when he writes – not only its actions – and a puppet's movements are limited – but the physical space in which it moves, taking care that what a puppet does and what he says reflect one another. 'The puppet is created to be mobile. Only when it moves does it become alive… The text has enormous importance, but if the words a puppet speaks do not correspond with its gestures, they become divorced from the puppet and hang in the air.' Further, as a puppet is characterised primarily by its gestures and movement, dialogue is written as part of these rather than to reflect its 'psychology', though this does not prevent the writer from giving the audience a sense of the puppet-character's mysterious inner being. It is also important that a writer grasps that a puppet play should revolve on a single emotional axis.

A writer can expect that language in puppet theatre may be inherently comical (Sherger, D & J, 1987). Merely the way a voice is produced in puppet theatre makes it comic. A single actor creating a variety of voices must use different accents, noises that are exaggerated and involving variations of tempo and pitch, as well as speech patterns that create stereotypes and caricatures that parody and mock actual language and which are designed to make the audience laugh. It may rely on improvisational verbal wit like punning, the use of 'patois' or innuendo and word-play for comic effect. The language of social and political satire or farce is particularly appropriate – a piece may deliberately flout language conventions (like Guignol's use of scatological language that was banned in Lyons, or Jarry's 'pschitt' that outraged the Parisian bourgeoisie). Because a puppet cannot be held responsible for its opinions and actions, it can subversively indulge in the carnivalesque letting off of steam.

Writing for Puppet Theatre Today

In Britain (rather than Europe, where puppet theatre is given greater weight) encouragement of writing for puppet theatre today is insufficient. 'Puppetry' is not only associated with children's theatre rather than theatre for adult entertainment, but as Helen Denniston pointed out in 1990 at the symposium on the training for puppeteers, 'puppetry' is often seen as 'a profession with low status, little artistic credibility and no academic underpinning' (Allen & Shaw, 1992). The picture is changing in Britain as funding is made available for creating performances of adult puppet theatre and for the touring of foreign companies using puppetry as an art-form for adult audiences, and critics are beginning to review it seriously. The form of 'theatre of animation' i.e. performance art in which several art-forms including that of puppetry co-exist in a single performance with writing, dance, sculpture, movement, acting, painting, costume design, and that includes animation of objects or acting figures, lives happily alongside modern dance, new circus, mime, physical theatre and live art.

There is a relative dearth of literary dramatic writing of adult puppet theatre today. This has several causes. Festival organiser Sharon Kivity (who is responsible for the bi-annual 'Visions' in Brighton, UK) points out that many modern touring animation theatre companies have minimal texts because of practical problems – commissioning a writer is an extra cost when the puppeteers can make do with substituting their own contributions. Translation of texts is another stumbling block: if a company tours the world it is easier to rely on visuals.

Helen Lannaghan, who organises the annual 'Festival of Mime' in London, feels that what puppeteers do best is manipulate puppets. They often do not have sufficient training to speak on stage and when they try to legitimise their production by including text, they fail to do so well enough. However, she does feel the situation is changing as the actor is becoming more centre stage in theatre of animation, and she included Michael Meschke's Marionetteatern's production of Roman Paske's adaptation of Strindberg's *A Dream Play* in the 1995 season, because of the quality of both acting and writing.

Few companies commission the writing of puppet theatre pieces for adults, though there are exceptions. (Movingstage Theatre Company, for example, commissioned the Howard Barker play included in this collection.)

Master-puppeteers see the problem as lying with writers who mostly write drama for 'live' actors rather than for puppets. The Central School of Speech and Drama's full-time training course in Puppetry in London, for example, now includes writers as part of the new training scheme. Writers are encouraged to create from scenarios that can be developed with a group of performers, where the technical features like the number and type of puppets used or the size of the stage, can be taken into account by the writer. In Europe and the USA, puppetry is underpinned by academic training and documentation, so writers are far more aware of the repetoire, and audiences are more receptive to puppet theatre as a serious art-form. A recent national enquiry into the state of puppetry in the UK and Ireland revealed that only 13% of puppeteers on courses had training in writing. (Allen & Shaw, 1992)

The 'Voice' of the Puppet

The speech of puppets is made to work differently on stage from that of 'live' actors. Finding ways in which the puppet's speech coincides with design and movement is important. Tillis points out that each type of puppet has its characteristic movement: 'String puppets can fly, but they cannot grasp objects or run – they must be whisked along…Hand-puppets can have fast and furious movements and cannot fly but…can swing an axe.' (Tillis, 1992)

In order to make the puppet appear more 'unhuman', certain techniques are used to lessen the disparity between the figure of the puppet and the 'voice' used by the puppeteer. One of these is to make the speaker visible on stage, so the onstage speaker and puppeteer interact, sometimes translating the puppeteer's voice into that of the puppet-character.

So that one actor can play several parts, puppet theatre may comically distort the voice using devices like the swazzle, taped voices, voices on microphones, or exaggeration or speech accents.

Conclusion

The fact of publication of this collection of plays written for theatre of animation, must declare a belief in encouraging the writing of texts for puppet theatre in a way that answers the medium's specific and exacting needs. It also declares a desire to preserve these texts, so that others can learn from them and so that they can form part of the puppet theatre repetoire.

The texts published here, express my belief as a playwright, that in the complex entirety of the puppet theatre as an art form, there is an important place for the writer. For centuries, from the Baroque to Barker, writers of excellence have been attracted to the special qualities of the medium (cf Appendix B). It is important that they are recorded in context of a performance to ensure that the tradition continues and that there is a modern repetoire from which new writers can learn. The puppet as metaphor for an 'object' that yet has life and consciousness breathed into it by the puppeteer working together with the audience, attracts writers who prefer writing for the puppet actor as 'alienated' rather than for the 'live' actor who works in realism or naturalism. The writing is about stylization and 'making strange', about entering into timelessness and mystery and the realm of 'grace, or the grotesque carnivalesque world of rude satire. It is also about writing for a performance that draws on several varied art forms from sculpture to song, from painting to acting, to attain the surprise, the beauty and the intensity of this very specialised art form.

References

Allen & Shaw. (1992) Editors. *On the Brink of Belonging.* p. 15. London. Calouste Gulbenkian Foundation.

Iglusias & Trutor. (1956) Editors. 'Les Entretiens d'Ostende'.

Jurkowski, H. (1979) Literary Views on Puppet theatre. In *Aspects of Puppet Theatre* (1988) edited by P. Francis. pp. 1–32. London: Puppet Centre Trust.

Jurkowski, H. (1991) 'Ecrivains et Marionettes: Quatres siècles de litterature dramatique en Europe'. pp. 58–64. Editions Institute International de la Marionette. Charleville-Mézières.

Kobialka, M. (1993) 'A Journey through Other Places: Essays and other Manifestos, 1994–1990'. Editor and Translator.

Obratsov, S. (1957) 'My Profession'. Moscow. Foreign Language Publication House.

Shaw, B. (1962) 'Complete Plays with Prefaces'. Vol 15. New York. Dodd, Mead & Co.

Segel, H. (1995) *'Pinocchio's Progeny'*. PAJ Books. John Hopkins University Press. Baltimore and London.

Sherger, D & J. (1987) Editors. *Humor and Comedy in Puppetry.* p. 1. Ohio. Bowling Green State University.

Speaight, G. (1990) pp. 183–190. 'The History of the English Puppet Theatre'. Robert Hale.

Tillis. (1992) *Towards an Aesthetic of the Puppet.* p. 6. USA. Greenwood Press.

Odd If You Dare

Nenagh Watson and Rachael Field
Song lyrics by Sylvia Hallett

Figure 1 DOO COT's *Odd If You Dare*. Photo: Ann McGuinness.

Contemporary Theatre Review
1999, Vol. 10, Part 1, pp. 15–30
Reprints available directly from the publisher
Photocopying permitted by license only

Odd If You Dare

SCENARIO

First Sequence: City Murder

The scene is set with three 'real' street lights placed on stage, two approximately 12ft apart stage left with the third placed opposite down stage right, a traffic light is placed upstage right. The centre stage has a back projection screen in four joined parts 10ft by 16ft. As the audience enter the traffic lights manually go through the usual sequence.

Darkness on stage.

TAPE of street noise is heard.

At a sound cue of a 'rushing sound' the outer screens are opened to reveal two illuminated city dresses – worn by two puppeteers. The dresses are constructed from scrap metal welded together on an open wire structure with the puppeteers standing inside them. The dresses have lights in them, they move forward on small wheels attached to the bottom frame. The screens close, and scratched super-8 film projection skims them to represent busy streets. The movements are like a mechanical ballet with each 'dress' being aware of the other but not relating directly to each other. This continues until a woman's voice on the tape says 'Go away, go away'. The screens open and 'dresses' turn and return to behind the screens.

The 'dresses' are placed directly behind the screens, MAGLITE (trade name) torches with the tops removed, are passed to the puppeteers. These are the light sources which are placed into the dress frame to produce shadow imagery on the screen, their detail is revealed and the streets became quieter and more sinister.

TAPE: The sound gets more frantic and the internal dress lights are switched off, the torch work continues until a woman's scream is heard on the tape, the torches zoom into one part of the frame, slowly moving down to rest. At the scream the red traffic light illuminates.

Stage right screen opens and the 'bigot' character enters dragging a body. He moves to centre of the screens up stage, lets the body fall, lets go and and roughly forces her head to face the audience. He corrects his hat and walks off towards the edge of the screen stage left. Before he exits, he glances at the body (this is momentary not lingering). *There is a silence.*

TAPE: Sound of emergency services.

From backstage, blue lights start to flash (the lights are the sort used in domestic burglar alarms wired to dry cell batteries), the two puppeteers place the lights into the dresses to create blue, flashing shadows, a large police light is also brought behind the screens, the MAGLITES are removed from the dresses at this point. The whole back stage and screens are now flooded with blue flashing lights echoing the sound of sirens. SINGER calls out through a megaphone: 'Stand back, make way for the ambulance. Stand back please. Make way, let the ambulance through.'

A puppeteer enters stage right. She has a role of police tape which she ties around lamp-post down stage right and continues across down stage to the opposite lamp-post attaching the end of the tape. The audience has been cornered off from the stage area. The puppeteer does not act a police woman but rather represents authority. A second puppeteer enters carrying a body-bag and approaches the body, the first puppeteer joins her and the body-bag is placed in front of the body. The body is then picked up and placed inside the body-bag. While this has been taking place, the singer has entered on stage right.

(The first verse of the opening song is sung through the megaphone)

SINGER: The city sleeps turning on its bad side.
A stranger enters from the shadow lands.
We feel our skin listening in the darkness,
the waves of fear when the devil spreads his hands –
lu la lay, lu la lu la lay, lu la lay, lu la lu la lay, lu la lay.

The two puppeteers place the body in the bag. The puppeteers lift the body bag and walk off stage left. As they leave the outline of the body appears (achieved with a body line gobo specially designed and made). SINGER puts down the megaphone and through a microphone continues with the song.

SINGER: (The blue flashing lights are turned off simultaneously.)
A house of bricks that now stands empty –
A hollow cave where we can call your name.
We strain our eyes to peer into the night,
lu la lay, lu la lay, lu la lay.

The silhouette is only seen in fire-light
so like a moth we'll head towards the flames.

How bright it burns when we have seen the shadows –
We will survive to celebrate our shame –
lu la lay, lu la lu la lay, lu la lay, lu la lu la lay lu la lay.

Molly enters stage left. She approaches the outline of the body. In her arms she carries a bouquet of flowers, not a grand bunch of flowers but the sort you buy at a market in shiny cellophane. In her grief she drops them onto the outline, and then collapses and weeps. A private moment of mourning.

Molly gets up and slowly returns backstage left, the singer who has completed her song, collects the megaphone and exits stage right. The stage is empty but for the bouquet. The first puppeteer enters and retrieves the police-tape and flowers. The city dresses are moved from the back of the screens to outside parallel on stage. They remain here throughout the performance.

Second Sequence: Runaway/Throwaway – Graveyard Birth

TAPE: From the discovery of her body and the murdered (distortion) after she disappeared (distortion) 5 months (distortion) recovery of her body and the weapon (distortion) she disappeared (distortion) her now (distortion) the long term (distortion)

As this is played, images appear on the screens of runaway and missing person posters (this is achieved with missing person posters which have been scanned into the computer and then printed on to acetate sheets. They are placed on two overhead projectors so that each image fills half the screen, crossing over with the images on the other projector, fading out simply by placing a handkerchief under the lens of the projectors. The final image is a missing poster of Ida, projected on to the screen stage right. This cross fades with the sound of a T.V. game show.)

TAPE: The sound of a T.V. game show, "Author of 1993 No. one best-selling novel, Peter?" Ida enters stage right. She is carrying a small cheap holdall in one hand and in the other she has a letter. She is full of indecision and worry.

TAPE: 'Pass' 'An anthology' 'From mythology: who was killed with a poison arrow in the heel?' 'Peter' 'Peccadillo?' 'Ten throng!' 'What new name was adopted in 1994 by the Spastic society?' 'All lose a crucial ten. It's Scope'. 'In 1994 which theatrical knight was accused of blasphemy after ripping a page..?' 'Peter' 'Guilgood'

Ida puts down the bag.

TAPE: 'No, Sir Ian Mc Kellan, lose ten. First published in 1946, whose book of baby and childcare had sold over Peter.'

A letter is projected onto right hand screen, which reads: 'Dear Mum and Dad, I just have to leave, please do not worry about me. Love from,'

TAPE: 'Stubs?' 'No, Dr Benjamin Spock.'

The projectionist writes onto the letter 'Ida'

TAPE: 'Lose ten. Who was the author of the 1987 booker prize winner'

Moon Tiger 'Carol?' (name lost with game theme tune and clapping).

Ida picks up her bag and exists.

Molly enters stage left. She is terrified.

TAPE: Violent angry male voice, it is very loud and distorted.

'Get back down over here, get back over here, get back down here, you little whore, get back down here whilst I'm still talking to you, you're no daughter of mine, get back down here, get back, you little whore, you tart, get back down here whilst I'm talking to you, get back, you're no daughter of mine.'

Cowering at the abusive voice, she moves down stage, returns to the screen up stage as if the screen (or her bedroom wall) will give her protection from the blows of the voice.

TAPE: 'What am I going to say to the people at work, what about your mother, what about your grandmother, how are you going to tell her, you little bitch, going around the town like a dog on heat, what am I suppose to do. Pack your bags and get out!'

At this point Molly's bag is thrown on stage from behind the screens.

TAPE: Get out you're no daughter of mine, I never want to see you again.'

Molly is hit by her bag being thrown out stage left. She retrieves the bag and searches in it for a small teddy bear and baby clothing, she cries into them, placing them back into the bag. This is under scored by;

TAPE returning to the game show: 'You both go home with a wonderful time-keepers, carriage clock, so thank you very much for being excellent contestants, Peter and Cathy!' Sound of clapping. 'Will you join me now for the final, the prize! Well done, fantastic performance, how are you feeling, are you feeling chuffed?' 'Yes!' 'Obviously for the first time in the programme she's speechless.' 'For the first time in my life!' 'Carol, here we are, congratulations, you are off to Africa and now let's just remind ourselves exactly where you are going...'

Molly, in pain, moves along down stage towards stage right, She falls, dropping the bag and rests against the lamp post. Ida enters stage right, She is in a hurry, so much so, she runs into Molly's bag. Molly pleads with her to help her, but Ida indicates that she cannot as she is in a hurry. This is a moment of struggle, full of emotion, lasting a few seconds only, but full of poignancy. Ida exits stage left, Molly gathers her bag and herself together and with struggle exits stage right.

The centre screens part, music is heard, the singer, who is a graveyard personified, is wheeled out. The screens close. The singer is wearing a cloth which is printed with photographic images of graveyards, around her neck hangs the small puppet body of an angel, with large white birds wings. It is placed so that the singers head appears to be that of the angel. She is standing on mobile steps to give her height, she has been placed by a puppeteer and stage manager. They check that her graveyard 'dress' is hanging correctly, in the manner of ladies in waiting, they then exit, one stage right the other stage left. As they exit, one puppeteer has put on the two overhead projectors, with identical photographic images of graveyards. These now fill the screens.

SINGER begins to sing the graveyard song, composed in the style of Hildegarde of Bingen.

SINGER: 'Blessed Lady
       rest in peace a while
       against my breast of stone
       cold and alone
       the sweet smell of flowers of death
       take away your pain.'

During the second verse, which is instrumental, Molly enters. She is obviously in pain, she clutches the bag to her stomach, she manages to find her way to the angel who looks down upon Molly, but does not respond directly to her. At the Angel's, feet Molly begins to deliver her child. The puppeteer has a carved baby concealed inside a bag, which is hidden underneath the body of Molly . As Molly 'gives birth' the baby is pushed through her skirt.

TAPE Sound of echoing church bells, mixing with the instrumental of the angels song.

Molly cradles the babe in her arms, and then with remorse and courage, places the babe in her basket. She then, with pain both physical and emotional, manages to get to her feet, she moves towards stage right, stops by the edge of the screen, she looks at her abandoned child. Into this picture enters a nun, stage left. Molly observes her and exits.

The nun is constructed from a sheep's skull and broken black umbrellas, with two umbrella handles as her feet. She enters slowly, sees the baby and shakes her head, looking out towards the audience.

SINGER: 'Angela de Mercici
       always looking for the answers
       she'll find your child, give her a home
       safe from temptation
       so pure and wise and free from sin
       she'll save your sinner's soul.'

The nun bends down, the puppeteer's arm, appearing as the nun's, picks the baby up in the bag and carries it away. As she returns back stage left, the projections of graveyards are faded out.

Third Sequence: Angel/Whore Transition

TAPE changes to cabaret music.

The Angel looks out towards the audience and winking teasingly at it, she places her hand under the graveyard dress and produces a Devil puppet, modelled very conscientiously on a 'Punch and Judy' style of Devil. It is a simple rod figure whose tail is like a phallus, the Angel animates the Devil exploiting the suggestive nature of the tail, the Devil is then left hanging whilst the Angel removes the angel puppet body from her neck. She creates the illusion that the body is flying, this is echoed by a puppeteer entering from stage left and taking the body from her, flying it towards a 'special' bright light up stage, exiting stage left. This should be a very beautiful moment.

The Angel then removes the graveyard dress, handing it to the stage manager who has entered stage right. Revealed is a 'sex' dress of bright red crushed velvet with at least 600 coloured condoms hanging from it.

Fourth Sequence: Strip

SINGER (The 'whore') now sings:
> 'Fallen Angel down from the sky
> don't need no feathers to make me fly.
> It may be wicked you may
> feel it's a con – don
>
> Sex for sale
> disposable dreams.
> I've got K.Y jelly and
> spermicidal creams.
> Is it a rip off or is it
> merely a con – don?
>
> I'm just a fabrication
> who needs your lubrication.
> You can stay up all night
> if you come with me.
>
> When sex is working it's an industry!'

As the song is sung 'Soho' projections fill the screens. (These are video grabs from a video of Soho reconstructed in the computer and printed onto acetate sheets, attached to a long acetate sheet which is then pulled along over the overhead projector, producing a filmic effect. During the song the images are static.)

At the end of the song 'When sex is working it's an industry', the centre screens open. One puppeteer takes away the steps closing the centre screens. The other puppeteer takes the microphone, placing it on its stand slightly off stage. Whilst this scene change is happening, the singer holds the stage and takes a bow and exists stage right.

TAPE: sound of a busy street.

The image projected now travels along. Into this image enters Ida from stage left. She is tentative and walks along as if in a Soho street. She stops at a projected sign saying 'Exotic dancers wanted', ponders it, and then exits stage right. A chair is bought out from stage right and placed down stage centre. The centre screens open and a gaudy slash curtain is placed in the gap.

TAPE: The sound moves to the interior of a club.

Into this the 'bigot' enters through the slash curtain and goes to the seat down stage. He shows off looking directly at the audience with an air of 'bonhomie', cocking his hat and generally feeling pleased with himself. Ida enters through the slash curtain and nervously stands within the centre area of screens and curtain.

TAPE: The 'stripper' music (David Rose) is played. It has been badly recorded deliberately.

Ida begins her routine. The stripper puppet is a carved torso with Ida's 'head', she is wearing a blond wig, with bits of her own ginger hair protruding, her costume is a black PVC bra top, the puppeteer's legs becoming her legs, wearing a shiny pink PVC mini skirt. As the routine progresses, the puppet removes the black top to reveal a 'Madonna' style pink glittery pointed bra. Ida moves towards the 'bigot' who is really enjoying the show. He grabs out at her but she quickly moves up stage centre. Ida turns her back on the audience to remove the pink bra, she turns around to reveal spinning tassels on her nipples.

This is too much for the 'bigot' who, in a state of over-excitement, leaps forward and grabs horridly at Ida's skirt. It rips off, Ida runs off stage left with the 'bigot' following. Ida re-enters from the slash curtain to retrieve her costume, exiting stage left.

TAPE: Resumes to outside sounds

The 'bigot' re-enters looking for Ida. He exits stage left. Ida in her 'day' clothes, with the strip costume hanging out of her shoulder bag, runs on from stage right. With the air of panic, humiliation, and fear, she exits stage left.

Silence.

Fifth Sequence: Park Scene

Three people enter (stage manager, singer, and puppeteer). They each take one of the lampposts and wheel it to form a parallel line down stage. The centre screens open. Molly who is sitting on the steps is pushed forward down stage. The screens are closed.

TAPE: Sound of composed 'bird song / park sounds'.

Projected images of line drawings depicting people in the park. (These are on two over-lapping sheets of acetate so that when they are moved, they give the illusion of life in the park.) Molly has hit hard times. Dejected and hungry, she sits in the park begging.

TAPE: The bird song becomes more composed and tuneful

A pigeon flies in from stage right, landing on the ground, down stage right, pecks at the ground. Molly notices pigeon and beckons, the pigeon hops back. Molly gets up and looks in the bin for some food then, after sitting back down, beckons to the pigeon again. This time the pigeon jumps on Molly's hand and their head movements echo each others. The pigeon opens its mouth and Molly shakes her head and the pigeon hops up over her head and flies off stage left. Ida runs in from stage left. She rests against a lamp post down stage left, looking over her shoulder, and then resuming to catch her breath. She does not notice Molly, for she is to preoccupied.

TAPE: There begins a faint threatening sound running underneath the park sounds.

The 'bigot' enters from stage left, he goes straight for Ida, who seeing him has begun to move towards stage right. She is terrified! Molly observing the whole situation, stands up and confronts the 'bigot' centre stage. The 'bigot' makes a move to down stage but Molly blocks his path. He then tries to get around her by moving up stage, but again Molly blocks his path. Molly then forces him to retreat back wards. He is forced to exit up stage left.

TAPE: The first motif from 'the circle' song is heard.

Molly signals to Ida that the coast is clear. Ida is amazed and extremely relieved and grateful, she moves to Molly and kisses her on the cheek. Molly is a little taken aback. They exit together stage left.

Sixth Sequence: Journey down

SINGER enters stage right and addresses the audience directly.

> 'Oh let us come in out of the cold
> been walking for hours
> worn through our souls.

I know for certain that you're there inside
peeped through net curtains trying to hide.

Let us in, we want a bed
and nothing more.
Let us in –
can't you hear us rapping
at your door?

Let us in, we want a bed
and nothing more.
Let us in –
can't you hear us rapping
at your door?

So it's no vacancies,
no room at the inn.
Just let us come in,
we're trying to smile
and I'm ringing your bell.
We try to talk nice
but you say go to hell.

Let us in, we want a bed
and nothing more.
Let us in
Can't you hear us rapping
at your door?
Can't you hear us rapping
at your door?

Wire images of Molly and Ida are projected onto the screens. Light source are Maglite torches. These shadow puppets are literally drawings of Molly and Ida's faces, but drawn with wire. The torch light is a movable source of light, the shadow images move around the screen, coming in and out of focus, changing in scale. The song continues. Door bells and rapping sounds come from back stage.
TAPE of composed 'drug music' begins to invade the song. Composed to evoke a feeling of loss of control, it creates a 'weird' atmosphere.

The shadows become more abstract and bizarre as the sequence progresses. Molly's shadow image fills the whole of stage right screen and then goes. Ida's shadow now really focuses into her face, particularly her eyes and gets as large as possible until it completely disappears. The puppet of Ida wonders out from stage left. She is not steady on her feet, and loses the support of her legs several times. Three people enter (as previously, stage manager, puppeteer and singer) and begin to move the lamp posts back to there original positions. This is done in such away as to appear as if they are moving in Ida's mind. She responds to them, trying to reach out for them. As she reaches, the lamp post is moved away. She clings to the lamp post held by the singer, but loses her grip and sways away towards the traffic lights. The sequence is going crazy. Ida staggers back to the centre of the screens. Projected images appear. Stage right is a collage of syringes. Stage left, a large syringe with liquid is aimed towards Ida. She reaches out for it. The liquid is expressed, Ida begins to feel a little more steady.

The projected images go. Molly enters stage left.

TAPE: The sound ends.

Ida holds out her hand, Molly shakes her head, Ida moves forward, head lowered. She is crying. Molly comes to comfort her, a moment of tenderness. However Molly leads Ida towards stage left and Ida leaves.

Seventh Sequence: Street

TAPE: There is the sound of cars passing.

Molly stands beneath lamp post downstage right. It is the only one illuminated. As the sound of a car is heard and we see head-lights move behind stage right screen. The lights wait, Molly responds by offering herself and walks off stage right.

TAPE the sound of a car door slamming.

The car lights move from the screen changing to rear red car lights and disappear. There is a moment of quiet.

TAPE the sound of a car returning, door slamming.

The car lights are repeated, Molly enters stage right, the car drives off. This sequence is repeated twice. On the third, Molly does not return so quickly.

During this gap the 'bigot' enters, obviously looking for a prostitute as he goes straight towards Molly's lamppost. He hovers around and then looks behind the edge of stage right screen, At this point Ida enters stage left, she is in a hurry, the 'bigot' turns around and they see each other. Ida turns to go, but the bigot moves towards her. He holds out his hand which has a twenty pound note in it. Ida shakes her head and looks forward down stage left. The 'bigot' comes up behind her and pushes his hand forward over Ida's shoulder so that the money is waved in her face. Ida shakes her head and moves across towards 'Molly's' lamp post, The 'bigot' pursues her and traps her against it, again pushing the money in her face. This happens three times, until Ida angrily forces past the bigot towards stage left. He pursues her, grabbing her shoulder. Ida turns and pushes him away, In so doing she drops her shoulder bag containing her strippers costume. Ida runs off stage left. The 'bigot,' centre stage bends down to Ida's bag, he caresses it, smelling a piece of the clothing, a ritualistic, horrid moment. As he stands, he places his hand on his groin (this must not be over done, but it must be clear what is going on). He looks around and leaves stage left.

Eighth Sequence: Dogs

Enter a small dog, stage right, (It is constructed from an old broom which is up-turned. It has a motor bike pedal and a bike pedal for legs, its face is a very small French metal sieve. It has one blue glass bead for its eye.) The singer also enters and stands at her microphone. The dog looks around and spots' Molly's lamp post, stage right, and then pees onto it – the singer is making the dog sounds. This small dog then sees Ida's bag and goes to smell it and bite at it. Another dog enters, stage left, he is slightly larger than the first, (Her body is an old road lamp set onto a small trolley which serves as legs, the head is an old 'pifco' lamp with 'Humberol' paint cans for eyes. Its teeth are pieces of a 'bow' saw blade) – it chases off the small dog, who exits stage right. This dog is cheeky and lively. If appropriate she begs at the audience and then goes to Ida's bag, smelling it. A slightly larger dog enters stage left, (His body is constructed from a rat cage. Its legs are cut pieces of blue hose-pipe with rope threaded through, with small light blue pulleys acting as paws. His head is made out of an old rusty 'Hurricane light', the eyes are the tops cut from aerosol cans). A loud bark is let out. This frightens the smaller dog, who looks up from the bag. They both move down stage centre, facing each other, They sniff and then they smell each other's 'bits', following around in a circle still smelling at each other. The small one breaks away, although the larger one is still smelling at her, the larger dog now mounts the smaller, 'mating' her centre stage. The larger dog disengages and smells at the other dog. Worried the whole procedure may happen again, the smaller dog quickly runs off stage right. The remaining dog looks out after the smaller, then licks its penis, goes to Ida's bag and smells at it, loses interest and lies down near it, stage left.

Enter a greyhound stage left. (Its body is constructed from two racks from the back of a bicycle, his legs are golf clubs, his head an old leather racing saddle from a bicycle with small car headlight bulbs representing eyes, a metal shoe horn is fixed in place for a mouth), The greyhound runs from one side of the stage to the other, and then spots the bag, the greyhound begins to go for it but the other dog lunges out at the greyhound.

SINGER has continued to bark and yelp in response to the dogs antics.

TAPE of wild dogs now joins the singers vocals, this builds up and takes over from the singer.

A monster dog enters stage right. (His body is an orange supermarket hand held shopping basket. Its legs are 'jump leads' with the grips acting as paws, its head is an old halogen security light wedged open with the gap forming a jaw and mouth, teeth are constructed from the 'bow' saw blade, its eyes are very small lights from the rear set of dynamo bicycle lights.) The three dogs leap into the air, with monster dog scarring the grey hound who exits stage right. The other two dogs face each other and leap up in the air, turning mid-air, landing in opposite positions, They leap at each other again, this time landing in the same place. Monster dog looks out menacingly at the audience, the other dog copies it. Monster dog then moves to the bag and begins to smell it. The other dog notices and goes for the bag. There is a struggle between them and the bag, in the process of this, the contents gets strewn out. They then go for the costume, smelling it and fighting each other off, While this is reaching a climax, the sound of a car screeching to a halt is heard and car head-lights flash into the screen. A car horn (air horn) is sounded and this frightens off both dogs, who exit stage left.

Molly enters stage right and sees the bag and contents strewn across the stage. She picks them up and grieves over them. Ida enters stage right, she sees Molly and is puzzled by her grieving. She quietly approaches her from behind and touches her on the shoulder. Molly's joy at seeing Ida is quickly turned to fear when Ida explains about her meeting with the 'bigot'. The two, quickly collect the stripper costume and bag and leave stage left as quickly as possible.

Ninth Sequence: Circle

SINGER enters stage right and starts to hum/la the love song.

A puppeteer and the stage manager move the three lamp posts to form a semi circle, placing one lamp post in the centre of the screens and the other two to the side of it. They exit either side of stage. Ida appears indicating to Molly that it is safe. They enter stage left. Ida goes directly into the centre of the circle and looking around within the circle, kneels down. Ida starts to trace the shape of the circle and as she does so, the circle fills with light.

SINGER: 'I use to draw a circle
                on the pavement round my feet
                tracing with my fingers

in the dirt upon the street.
People in the cesspit don't know they're going down
I watch them from my circle, my home inside this town.'

Ida looks up to Molly who begins to walk around the outside of the circle.

SINGER: And I've been waiting for a love like this
I've been waiting for the waters to subside.
And I've been waiting for a love like this
To feel safe here inside.'

Molly is now back resting against the lamp post stage left. She is focused on Ida who has now stood up and is looking out towards the audience.

SINGER: 'I dreamed I saw a pigeon
Wading out towards the storm.
Its wings were torn and shattered –
Picked it up and brought it home.'

Ida faces Molly and reaches out, drawing her into the circle, they very slowly begin to dance together.

SINGER: 'Home is where the heart is and the rain keeps coming down.
We'll shelter in this doorway
And keep each other warm.
And I've been waiting for a love like this
I've been waiting for the waters to subside.
And I've been waiting for a love like this
To feel safe here inside.'

Ida and Molly are now facing each other. Ida lowers to her knees, reaching up to Molly, who moves down to face her, they embrace. The two huddle in the centre of the lamp posts. The song ends, the singer exits stage right, leaving Molly and Ida to sleep.

Tenth Sequence: The Dream

Molly starts to get restless.
TAPE: Strange religious music, composed to sound like a very cheap organ mixed with wind up musical boxes.
Images are revealed of the Madonna and nuns. These are projected on the screens. Molly seeing these images stands in reverence. The nun enters stage left and beckons to Molly. She produces Molly's baby from underneath her habit and holds it out for Molly. Molly reaches out for it

Figure 2 Doreen Edwards sings the 'Graveyard Song' in DOO COT's *Odd If You Dare*. Photo: Ann McGuinness.

and then remembers Ida and goes back to her. The nun beckons again and Molly reaches out and again returns to Ida. The nun beckons again and this time Molly reaches out and begins to follow the nun as she moves off stage. Molly gives the sleeping Ida a final look and exits.

Eleventh Sequence: Murder

TAPE: The tape played at the beginning of the performance is repeated.

Two lamp post are moved by the stage manager and the singer, leaving the up stage centre one. Ida is alone and vulnerable. The 'bigot' enters stage right, looking at the sleeping Ida. He hovers over her.

TAPE: The sounds of breathing and a woman's voice saying 'GO AWAY'.

Just before the words the 'bigot' reaches out pushes Ida down. Ida looks up at the bigot.

TAPE: 'GO AWAY' is heard.

Ida struggles to her feet. She rushes forward, looking out in fright towards the audience stage left. The 'bigot' comes up behind her. She moves away, running to the lamp post down stage, The 'bigot' pins her against it. She in terror looks at him, he caresses her face, she is terrified, pushes him away moving back towards stage left. The 'bigot' lashes out, knocking her down. He hovers over her, but she gets to her feet and dashes to down stage left. The bigot follows, Ida rushes towards centre stage, the bigot grabs her from behind, forcing her down. He moves over her, forcing himself down upon her.

TAPE: A distorted male voice too distorted for words to be audible.

The 'bigot' 'rapes' Ida.

TAPE: The distorted voice sounds out again.

Ida manages to lift her head up to plead with the 'bigot', the 'bigot' is getting out a knife which he now holds above her.

TAPE: A woman screams.

The 'bigot' lowers the knife and stabs Ida, her body contorts. The 'bigot' gets up, cocks his hat and exits stage right. Silence, slow fade to blackout. The puppeteer gets up and removes Ida's body, exiting stage left.

Twelfth Sequence: Finale

A silent film is projected up of the smashed and murdered images of Ida.

TAPE: A loud soundtrack crashes in, it is based on the opening song, but in the style of American 'riot girls' (post punk).

The projected images 'film' is turned off. A slide projector is turned on and goes through a sequence of images from a pathologist. The line drawing of the body seen at the beginning is projected centre stage, echoing Ida's broken body.

SINGER enters stage right and goes to centre stage.

SINGER: 'The city sleeps, turning on its bad side.
　　　　A stranger enters from the shadow lands'

Two puppeteers enter stage right and left and grab microphones – all three sing the chorus 'We'll survive…'

ALL: 'We'll survive remembering the bad side,
　　　We'll survive to celebrate our shame.'

SINGER: 'We feel our skin listening in the darkness –
　　　　Waves of fear as the devil spreads his hands
　　　　And the blood flows down, down.'

ALL: 'We'll survive remembering the darkness,
　　　We'll survive to celebrate our shame.'

SINGER: 'The silhouette is only seen in firelight,
　　　　So like a moth we'll head towards the flames
　　　　And our wings will burn, burn.'

ALL: 'We'll survive remembering the shadows,
　　　We'll survive to celebrate our shame.'

SINGER: 'As the violence cuts into us we fight for air
　　　　And the terror sucks us in as we watch it on the screen –
　　　　The fascination dares us to confront our deepest fears.'

ALL: 'And we bleed and we cry and we watch it again in our
　　　minds eye –
　　　We have killed, we have murdered in our minds eye –
　　　So we can remember.
　　　We'll survive so we can remember –
　　　We'll survive to celebrate our SHAME.'

THE END

Contemporary Theatre Review
1999, Vol. 10, Part 1, pp. 31–33
Reprints available directly from the publisher
Photocopying permitted by license only

Parthenogenesis, Parentage and Creation of DOO COT

Nenagh Watson and Rachael Field

'They hunched up into their puppets, their eyes like dark fireballs so lost, so focused. They sighed and breathed into them, shared their arms and their bodies and a times, it seemed, their very souls.'

Nicola Barker, The Observer.

How did it all begin? Ten years ago we both exhibited work in a Lesbian art exhibition. During the installing of it, we met and that's the beginning.

Our work, individually and collaboratively is created and drawn from our lives, often autobiographical but also inspired by stolen true stories of lives around us. Life is a duality of beauty and despair and so is our art.

It is our love of cities, the urbanization, the backs of factories and the insides of cathedrals, the vivid mix of cultures and the resulting creativity which gives extra appeal to living and working in Manchester. It has been our home for over ten years and is a challenging and disturbing place to work.

Puppeteer – Nenagh Watson

In constructing the puppet figures Watson uses discarded objects combined with fabricated elements. She feels that a discarded object has a previous existence that accompanies it, etched within by usage of time. Urban waste echoes its environment and aligns to analogies of city life. The discarded is rescued, revived by recontextualization but not wholly transformed, adding to its poignancy and humour.

'It struck me at the time, and strikes me still, that to be able to create objects of such extraordinary ingenuity and beauty out of scrap is talent enough, but to create live magic around them, too, is simple genius.'

Nicola Barker, The Observer 22nd May 1994.

Creation of the illusion of life from an inanimate object is a constant exploration within Watson's work. The roots of the puppet figure lie within the tradition of shamanism, with superstition still echoing ancient fears of blasphemy and possession.

'The final blasphemy – that of creating the illusion of life. The flamboyant opposition of death and life, of the artificial and the real.'
> Simon Pummell (on the Films of Ladislaw Starewicz), Sight and Sound, May 1995.

Duality of making and performing have continued to be of equal importance. The theatre of puppets is essentially a theatre of integration – the ultimate in cross-disciplinary work.

Painter – Rachael Field

'The bold figurative paintings of Rachael Field have a monumental quality describing the private sphere of women's lives with a broad political and public structure…The individual support within collective action is powerfully expressed.'
> Emmanuel Cooper, The Sexual Perspective, Routledge, 1994.

Field is currently exploring computer animation to make painting work in the hypermedia. Collecting visual and aural material – like notes for a book – reconstructing information via the computer. It needs raw input – communication through the wire – a broad stroke of paint in the minutiae of the microchip. Fat paint and thin chips. She is experimenting with how painting can be brought to life and taken back into performance. Field believes that moving images show more emotion and can even convey the experience of the subjects. By moving through a portrait into what is in the head, we can literally show thought processes. To see the layered images inside the head, visualising the difference between what is real and what is imagined. The real and unreal mingle.

"A fully understood idea is a dead idea. My work has taught me that places of shadow are far more interesting than fully illuminated rooms."
> Bill Viola, unpublished notes on 'The Passing' quoted in 'rites of passage' catalogue
> Tate Gallery.

Field's exploration of shadow images brings the intensity of her monumental paintings, her love of colour into the theatre, by literally filling screens with light, colour and often live painting. Her compositional eye sees the stage space as a huge canvas, where by paintings are given the freedom to move and literally breath. It is her vision as painter which has informed and challenged DOO COT's work stealing from the language of the fine artist to give a unique overview of the stage space. She describes her approach to theatre as 'mark-making,' adopting the European term 'scenography' translated as 'drawing in air'. The stage space a canvas with each intrusion; puppet, actor, music, sound, light equating to a mark. The total equality of the different elements which go to create the final piece is paramount. It is an art of radical juxtaposition.

'An extraordinary fusion of painting, object and figure manipulation, live and recorded music, shadows and most recently computer animation.'

Stella Hall, The rise and rise of DOO COT, Animations, May 1995.

Collaboration is a process of conflict, it is born out of struggle, but one which sheds new light on each other's working process eventually creating a hybrid. It is the ultimate in artificial procreation. DOO COT seek out other collaborators who contribute on a project basis. Sylvia Hallett composes with sounds stolen from the street, lyrics become haunting melodies and strange ditties.

Contemporary Theatre Review
1999, Vol. 10, Part 1, pp. 35–39
Reprints available directly from the publisher
Photocopying permitted by license only

Notes on Puppetry as a Theatrical Art: Response to an Interview

Eric Bass

A puppet is, of course, an object, and, of course, one that is animated, or manipulated, performed with. Beyond this, it is a reflection of the human state of being, a bizarre mirror, an "other". It may take a somewhat human form, or it may be quite abstract, but it never sees the world quite the same way as a human would. This may not exactly "define" the puppet, but it is, I think, the point of the puppet. It is a theatrical object which invites us, the human audience, to see ourselves through very different eyes.

Using this "definition", it follows that I am most interested in the puppet together with the human actor; that is, in presenting the human's encounter with this "other". This theatrical context also gives the puppet a role: it becomes a memory, a nightmare, a wish, a ghost, an answer to a question. Although some puppet traditions, notably the Indonesian, understand a certain spiritual quality in the puppet, most of them use the puppet (at least visually speaking) primarily within its own world. Combining the puppet's world and ours (if we are each true to our own world) begs a confrontation with this strange reflection: it is Punch speaking to the audience, in which the audience is also part of the play.

One of the functions of theater is, certainly, to give us, the audience, a different look at ourselves, to be a magic mirror. A puppet, used properly, embodies this concept. Before the first word of the play is spoken, we see that we are not looking at life through usual eyes. We have met the theatrical equivalent of a man from Mars, or a Golem, or a hallucination. This is not to say that the puppet "portrays" this other. It is other, no matter what it tries to be. The theatrical power of any puppet, whether a miniaturized man in a bottle or a giant pageant creature, is in its keeping true to its nature as puppet. The laws of puppet nature are different from ours. As a non-living object, the puppet, brought to life, is always a metaphor. It's nature, therefore, is metaphorical. Whatever the specific character of a puppet, its nature, fundamentally, cannot be betrayed. When the puppet and the human actor confront each other, it is the nature of the human that comes into question.

Often, in puppet theater, a puppet's character is conveyed by its expression. This is especially true in some folk traditions where, for instance, a robber will be created with a particular "robber-like" grimace. I prefer a puppet whose character is strong, but whose expression is neutral; that is, the puppet has all the sculptural elements of a character, but the eyes and the mouth are neither staring nor distorted. Such a puppet seems to be able to change expressions, without changing character. It becomes more of an actor. At the same time, a puppet is always part of the scenography, part of a picture, even if the background is black. We know that the puppet is a creation of a human hand, so we look for the context for which it was made. An actor can often be looked at out of context, because, as a human, he is subjective, just as we are, the individual viewers. The puppet needs to be seen as a moving part of a larger image. It is a representation, a depiction, and the sensation that it seems to be alive creates a theatrical tension. Its very presence seems to imply the world or picture to which it belongs.

Some theorists talk about using the actor as a puppet. What might they mean by this? Could it mean to stylize his movements? To diminish his freedom of choice, his will? I think the deeper sense of this idea is to bind the actor to a stage picture, so that he is perceived as an animation of a world, and one which is not ours. And by saying the world is not ours, I mean that the world we see is a metaphorical world, not a literal "outer space". Essentially, the puppet is a metaphor.

Most of the texts which I use for puppets are created through dialogue between my idea of a particular puppet character and my sense of what the puppet "wants" to do. There seems to be, in the best of puppets, a choice that that puppet needs to make. Its character, its function (what job it was built to do), its scale, its aesthetic and even the tradition it comes from all lead it down a path. It seems to perceive in a certain way, and to react accordingly. I see my job as that of trying to find this sense of a puppet, and to "let it do" what it wants, to make its own choice. If I have a specific text for the puppet, I might have to change it to suit the puppet, or change the puppet to suit the text. I try to remember that the puppet is a metaphor for some aspect of the text, or an embodiment of an image of the text. At the same time, if I want the puppet, the image, the metaphor to "live", I need to find the "life" it already contains. In some cultures, this might be regarded as a spiritual handling of the object. In a more mundane vein, it can be seen as research, but using the senses rather than just the mind. Using my senses "on behalf of the puppet" helps me find the senses, the "life", of the puppet. This also suggests that the puppet is free to improvise, in the sense that all performance is in some way improvised, because no two moments are the same. But whether that improvisation can extend itself beyond the limits of the text or the scene depends on the whole context, the style and aesthetic, of a piece. In some pieces, with some characters, it is appropriate; in others, not.

When I think of manipulating a puppet, I think of it breathing. In the human, no natural movements can be divorced from the breath. I try to work from the center of the puppet, not from its limbs, and to connect that center to my own breathing, bringing my breath down to the proportion of the puppet. I find it helpful not to think of moving the puppet at all, but to think of filling or emptying the puppet with a hope or a desire, or a despair or fear. These hopes and despairs take the form of breath, so the movement of the puppet always begins in its center, and is always connected directly to a motivation. I cannot use the puppet as an automaton. Perfection, for me, is found in an uninterrupted sense of the puppet's being, not in its movements.

Naturally, I have to use puppets that are designed to be used as I want to use them. In a three-dimensional figure, there needs to be room in the body for this "breath"; i.e. there needs to be a degree of play in the structure, an ability to collapse somewhat, so that the filling and emptying of the puppet is visible. I credit the Japanese Bunraku theater as an inspiration, but my puppets are generally manipulated by only one manipulator, and usually stand about 20 inches high, or less. I like smallness in puppets, mostly for the intimacy they invite, and the focus they require. I want the design of the puppets to be consistent with my preference for theater that does not impress or jump out at the audience, but invites a kind of quiet complicity.

Because the audience knows that the puppet is not really alive, it has to invest life in the puppet. In a sense, the audience is as much the manipulator of the puppet as the puppeteer is. The puppeteer, by means of his or her skill in performance, can make the invitation for the audience to invest. When the invitation is accepted, the puppeteer, puppet and audience have formed a bond; they are indispensible to each other. This seems to me to be a natural potential of puppet theater, and one which it can perhaps do better than any other form of theater.

The perception of the puppet as "other" and the need for the audiences's complicity in giving the puppet "life" suggest that the puppet cannot really imitate life as we humans know it. Although there are theatrical conventions in which the puppet does try to imitate the human world, I believe they go against the puppet's nature. This does not mean that a puppet cannot play a "human" character; it means that in playing the human, the puppet will not be imitating life, but reflecting it, as if from another dimension. In playing a human, the puppet gives us distance from our subject, even at the same time that it might draw out our emotions; but what we feel for the little "imitator of life" might not be identification. It might be compassion.

This might be seen as a "poetic" approach to puppet theater, but "poetic" is rather a deadly word in theatrical contexts. It often implies something obscure, not for the masses, even humourless. And so, rather than say this approach is poetic, I would call it metaphorical. As metaphors are the stuff of which poems are made, they are also the stuff of which dreams are made, and the stuff which shows us another side of any "reality". Within metaphor, there can be satire, fantasy, character and exaggeration. What is important is that "this" is seen as "that"; the "that" can be any image or puppet that rings true to the creator.

I believe that most audiences like a good story, but that a story can be told or implied by many means, including presentation of a collection of images. In assembling the images, the audience reads the story into them, or fills in the spaces between the scenes. What role does the puppet have in this? Above all, I like the puppet to be a presence; an object, emanating a seeming consciousness of the larger space around it. I need to experience the puppet in relation to something. If the puppet has a sense of the vastness around it, for example, I understand its relation to something, even if I see it standing alone. This presence gives life to the entire picture. In a sense, the puppeteer is not manipulating the puppet, but is, through the puppet, manipulating the puppet's world, an environment. It is the creation of this world which is important to me. Metaphorically speaking, creating a truly full entity of one puppet can create a world.

I cannot imagine designing a puppet outside of the full aesthetic of the world of which the puppet is part. I build a puppet to live in a specific piece and to interact with all the elements of that piece: actors, masks, stage. If the piece involves the meeting of different worlds, the design of the puppet needs to make this both clear and possible. I take into account the scale of the puppet, what functions it needs to manage, its character, and its scale, in relationship to the world around it. Then I decide on a design for its mechanics and form. I generally take a rather human form and put together some combination of techniques from the various rod-puppet traditions and Bunraku, but not necessarily. Most important is the reason for having the puppet at all. I think that even within the art of puppet theater, the puppet must justify its own existence. It is not enough to choose a puppet for a piece simply because I am a puppeteer. I have to understand what is being said by the use of the puppet, what metaphor is being served. Is the puppet, for instance, in the mind of a human actor? If so, what is the imagination of the actor's character like? I like puppets with human characteristics, ones that can play a role in human memory or dreams. I work to keep the puppets' expressions neutral, while letting their characters come through, and hope that those characters speak to me even at the workbench, helping to develop the piece.

Some puppets are made to speak, others are not. Some seem to have a voice within them; in others, no voice can be found. I think it is part of the job of a puppeteer to discover what voice, if any, his or her puppet has. Separating the speaking puppet from the actual voice (e.g. having an offstage speaker) reminds the audience that the puppet is only a puppet, which can add to the style of a puppet performance. There is also, however, a magic in building the illusion that the puppet is truly speaking, and then breaking the illusion by having the puppet remind us that he is only a puppet (which in turn builds the illusion). I have played with both of these approaches. I do not think that either is preferable, or more distinctive, as a rule. What I most like about theater is that each production sets its own rules; I only insist that the production be consistent within its rules, and that the rules be organic to the complete aesthetic of the production.

We often praise ourselves and others for all the marvelous things we can do. We praise the puppet because it can defy gravity, transform itself. I like the puppet for its limitations, for what it is too small to reach, or because it is too attached to its manipulator to be independent. The puppet can be a metaphor for just those limitations, which can make it both more human and more heroic. We can love the puppet for what it fails to achieve. I wouldn't mind if we could extend this compassion to ourselves.

Nuptial Night

A Surrealist Comedy

Written and translated from the Finnish
by Johanna Enckell

The first performance of HÄÄYÖ (title in Finnish) was given at
TEATTERI MUKAMAS in Tampere, Finland, on 19 February 1994. It was
directed by Johanna Enckell, and the décor was inspired by René
Magritte and built by Anna-Liisa Takala. The cast was as follows:

MAJA	Anna Lihavainen
ADAM / MAX etc.	Vesa Pekkanen
THE PARROT'S SOUL etc.	Jukka-Pekka Miettinen

Figure 3 Noah's Ark stranded upon Mount Ararat in Johanna Enckells's *Nuptial Night*. Anne Lihavainen as Maja. Photo: Vesa-Ville Saarinen.

Contemporary Theatre Review
1999, Vol. 10, Part 1, pp. 43–55
Reprints available directly from the publisher
Photocopying permitted by license only

Nuptial Night

A Surrealist Comedy

Actors	Maja the Bride Father / Adam / Modern man / Max Mother / The Parrot's Soul (also Musician)
Puppets	A White Bird A Parrot Maja the Baby Noah Adam's Great Family (Baby-dolls that can be wound up.)
A Mask	"The Rape" of Réné Magritte
Main objects	A big black bowler A normal size bowler A small bowler

Puppets and objects can also be made by the actor's hands and fingers: Noah (a finger), THE MONSTER in the WC (a white-gloved hand), THE PARROT (two hands in green and red gloves) etc.

Scenography   A room by Réné Magritte with a staircase that leads nowhere. There is a frame on the wall. Behind the frame is a small stage. In the room there is a water closet, through which the puppeteer can show or throw up things.

The action takes place in a bachelor's flat.

I

Out of the darkness flutters a white bird.
The bird flutters as if against an invisible glass.
Suddenly it disappears.

In its stead there lies a white bride on the floor. It is Maja. She is seven months pregnant. Arranged around her is a wedding bouquet and a Bible.
A strange sound wakes her up.

MAJA: Where am I?

A white insect-like creature appears in the WC.
Then it disappears.

MAJA: Max!

A Parrot perches on the wall.

THE PARROT: Darling!
MAJA: Max, come here!
PARROT: Max! Darling! Max! Darling!
MAJA: Max, you can't do this to me!

Maja strolls around, picks up Max's toothbrush.

MAJA: I'll throw your toothbrush in the WC!

She looks at the toothbrush and finds that it is a shoebrush. She drops it in the WC. The Parrot imitates the sound of the brush falling into the water.
Then Maja starts out for Max's bowler hanging on the wall. She puts the bowler on her head.

MAJA: Max, now I'll take your sacred bowler.
PARROT: Bloody Mary! Bloody Mary! Bloody Mary!
MAJA: Shut up!

She throws her wedding bouquet at the parrot.

MAJA: That bird's driving me crazy!

She throws herself on the floor.

MAJA: Max, it's not fair to leave me alone on our wedding-night. I can
    hear my poor heart beating.
PARROT: This is the manic-depressive type.
MAJA: Max, who taught that parrot to speak? Idiot!
PARROT: Idiot! Idiot!
MAJA: It's getting on my nerves.
PARROT: Take it easy. Relax. Take it easy. Relax.
MAJA: Max, please, where are you?

The wedding bouquet is thrown back to Maja through the WC.

PARROT: Darling. I love you, only you, Nina!
MAJA: Nina? Max! Who is Nina!
PARROT: Nina, kiss me, oh Nina, kiss me, kiss me!

Maja takes her little blue suitcase and starts for the door.

MAJA: I've had enough, Max. I am going to quit, Max. It is not you who
are leaving me, Max. I am now leaving you, Max.

*She is about to dash up the stairs when she realises that there is no way out. She
falls on the floor at the foot of the staircase.*

MAJA: What does all this mean?

Now the Parrot changes its voice and becomes friendly.

PARROT: Please tell me your name, What's your name?
MAJA: Oh! Maja. My name is Maja.
PARROT: Where do you come from?
MAJA: From Tulse Hill. Max and I met in April at Punta del Sol.
  And then…well…well…
PARROT: Oh, Lola! Lola! Lola! Welcome Lola!
  Kiss me, Lola! Kiss me!

Maja dashes up the stairs and grabs the parrot by its throat.

PARROT: Take your time! Take your time!

*Choked sounds from the Parrot. It falls dead behind the wall. Maja sinks down
on the floor. Now there appears from behind the wall the man-sized light-green
soul of a parrot in a jogging suit.*

THE PARROT'S SOUL: She strangled me! So now I am among the dead.
This must be freedom. Yes, I am free. Well, I am just the poor light-
green soul of a parrot. No need to shed tears or to get upset. This can't
be called a murder. Can it? Just a poor parrot. But look at her! She is
unhappy. She is suffering. Oh dear, oh dear!

What the Parrot's soul asks for is thrown out of the WC

THE PARROT'S SOUL: Give me a potato!

A potato is thrown out of the WC. He catches it.

                    Give me a tomato!

A tomato is thrown out of the WC. He catches it.

                    Give me some corn!

Some corn is thrown out of the WC. He catches it.
He mixes a drink

PARROT'S SOUL: A Bloody Mary for you.

Maja drinks it all.

The Parrot's soul turns towards the WC and plays his flute, and very slowly, up from the WC comes a baby's arm. Maja crawls towards the WC and takes the baby's arm and feels how it caresses her cheek.

MAJA: I have the feeling that it likes me.

A baby's head comes up from the WC, falls to the floor and rolls around. Maja picks it up. The Parrot's soul continues to enchant the WC with his flute and then the whole body (without head and arm) of a baby-doll rises from the WC. Its only arm is raised (as the Goddess of Liberty.) Maja lifts her arm likewise and goes towards the baby-doll and takes it carefully in her lap. Now Maja tries to put together the pieces of the baby-doll.

MAJA: I remember those days…
PARROT'S SOUL: Let us all remember those good old days of the past!

Parrot's soul disappears behind the stage.

II

The small stage behind the frame is lit, and Maja is in the bachelor's flat looking towards the frame:

MAJA'S MOTHER'S VOICE: Maja! Maja! Can you hear me, Maja? Answer me!
MAJA: Can I hear you! I hear nothing but you, Mother.

Maja's Mother's head appears within the frame.

MOTHER: Inside immediately before Daddy wakes up!
MAJA: No.
MOTHER: Be careful, Maja. The cold will make you a cripple. Or you will freeze to death. Then Mummy and Daddy will have to put their little Maja in a coffin. Down in the cold cellar with her. And then we'll bury her deep into earth. Do you hear me Maja?
MAJA: Oh, I'm so cold. I'm freezing so much. My heart is squeezed and crippled, put into a coffin deep down in the earth. Oh, how I'm freezing!

Her Father's voice is heard from behind

FATHER'S VOICE: Coffee!
MAJA: That's him. That's Daddy!

Her Father's head appears in the frame. He wears a bowler hat and he is reading the morning paper.

MOTHER: Say something!
FATHER (*reading*): My God.
MOTHER: Yes?
FATHER: Total crash on the stock market.
MOTHER: That's beside the point.
FATHER: So it says in the paper.
MOTHER: What the paper says doesn't matter to me.
FATHER: That's a shame.
MOTHER: Shame on you! You-you-you…pig!
FATHER: Coffee please.

Mother pours the coffee with a trembling hand. Silence.

MOTHER: Where have you been all night?
FATHER: What?
MOTHER: Where? I'm asking you where?
FATHER: What do you mean: 'where'?
MOTHER: I said: Where have you been all night.
FATHER: Me?
MOTHER: Yes, you.
FATHER: What night?
MOTHER: Don't try!
FATHER: I'm not trying.
MOTHER: So you aren't trying!
FATHER: What?
MOTHER: What! What! What!
FATHER: A screw's loose.
MOTHER: You're as slippery as an eel!

Father flings his newspaper away.

FATHER: I'm leaving. Goodbye!
MOTHER: Mind the doorstep!

The door slams shut.

MAJA: Daddy!
MOTHER: Herbert! Don't do it again!

Maja tries to comfort her Mother.

MAJA: Oh, Mummy…
MOTHER: Shut up! Don't touch me! Oh, Herbert…

Mother cries and sings an old love song from her happy days. She slowly disappears. The Parrot's soul comes in from behind.

PARROT'S SOUL: There it was, the good old style from the good old days.

MAJA: I promise – Never again.
PARROT'S SOUL: But that's how it is. That's life.
MAJA: Never, never again.

The Parrot's soul grabs the Bible from the floor.

PARROT'S SOUL: Swear on the Bible!
MAJA: The Bible is not for parrots.

The Parrot's soul looks into the Bible, reads.

PARROT'S SOUL: Oh, there are so many lives, so many souls. I am sure
   the Bible takes parrots into consideration…

The Parrot's soul gets very close to Maja.

PARROT'S SOUL: A nice pair of parrots!
MAJA: On my wedding night I do not want to be attended upon by a
   dead parrot. Max dear, please come now!
PARROT'S SOUL: Can't you put Max out of your mind?
MAJA: He will be here in a minute.
PARROT'S SOUL: Out of where?
MAJA: I trust him.

The Parrot's soul grabs a pair of scissors and points them towards Maja.

PARROT'S SOUL: Trust me. I'm your doctor.
MAJA: Max, please come and rid me of this monster! Do please tell this
   soul of a parrot that you are the doctor.
PARROT'S SOUL: Max is a bachelor by profession.
MAJA: I can't stand this any longer. What is all this about?
PARROT'S SOUL: This is a bachelor's flat.
MAJA: A bride in a bachelor's flat? What kind of a future will that
   make?
PARROT'S SOUL: The good old story once again. Let's see..

*The Parrot's soul makes magic signs over Max's bowler and out of it pop two
paper cutouts, true copies of Maja's parents.*

MAJA: Mummy and Daddy! No! Not them!

The Parrot's soul forces the Mother and Father on her.

PARROT'S SOUL: Now, be a good girl, take Daddy in your left hand
   and Mummy in your right hand. That's it. Tell me, what will happen?

Maja imitates her parents. She speaks for the two paper cutouts.

MAJA: – Where have you been all night?
      – A screw's loose.

> – You're as slippery as an eel!
> – I'm leaving! Goodbye!
> – Herbert!

(*In a small voice*) Mummy..

> – Shut up! Don't touch me!

Maja turns towards the audience with the paper cutouts lifted.

MAJA: This is the sad story about a Mummy who never stopped yelling at me. Not until I turned her into a little crumpled ball of paper.

Maja crumples her Mummy and tosses the little ball of paper in the air. The Parrot's soul catches it and tosses it far away.

MAJA: And this is the sad story about a Daddy…

Parrot's soul hands her a pair of scissors.

> … whom I hardly saw, hardly knew.

Maja cuts off Daddy's head.

> Daddy lost his head, bowler and all!

III

A Tango at a high volume. An enormous black bowler on two legs in a pair of shiny men's shoes enters. The legs move along in Tango steps. Suddenly the music stops and the bowler drops to the floor in the middle of the Bachelor's flat.

MAJA: It's only a hat.

Sound of drums. On top of the bowler is a big hand which catches a small finger. They disappear into the bowler.

MAJA: Ghastly secrets.

The hand is back on top of the bowler. Now it points at Maja.
A Voice from within the bowler:

VOICE: A mammoth mammal animal!
MAJA: Can I really stand all this? No! I'm fed up. I'm still young. I want a happy life. I'm leaving.

Once again she picks up her little suitcase, once again she reaches the staircase only to realize, once again, that there is no way out. She drops her little blue suitcase and falls down at the foot of the staircase.

Parrot's soul has caught hold of the brim of the bowler. He wants Maja to come and help him to lift the bowler.

PARROT'S SOUL: This is the moment of fate and destiny.
MAJA: It might be dangerous.
PARROT'S SOUL: Stay with me. Live dangerously.

Maja is tempted by the danger. Together they try to lift the bowler. It begins to tremble and moves along the floor. They try again. They place the bowler brim down. In front of the big bowler they discover a man wearing a bowler and dark sunglasses. He remains without moving till the light is on him. Then he begins to polish his shoe with a mechanical rhythm.

MAJA: Is it…Max?

The man continues to polish his shoe.

MAJA: Daddy?

The man polished his shoe as before.

MAJA: It seems as if he didn't notice me at all.

At last the man finishes polishing his shoe, puts the shoe-brush in his pocket and moves in a peculiar way on his knees on to the frame that now becomes a window. A curtain rises, reveals a blue sky with small white clouds. The man with the bowler looks out of this window. Silence.

MAJA: I have a feeling that this man is a very, very lonely man.

The man now turns towards the WC. Slowly the man bends down with his head in the WC.

MAJA: Might there be a hole in his heart?
PARROT'S SOUL: What do you mean? It's not at all relevant.

When he is out of the WC bowl the man begins to speak.

ADAM: I have a great family. I'm Adam.
MAJA: Oh, hello, I'm Maja. I'm from Tulse Hill and me and Max, you
     know, we met in Punta del –
ADAM: For God's sake. Let it be.
MAJA: I presume you would like to tell me about your great family?
ADAM: My family is a long story.
MAJA: Go on. I believe I have all the time in the world.

Adam sits down behind the big bowler and Maja makes herself comfortable in front of it. The Parrot's soul climbs the staircase to fetch a mask.

IV

ADAM: In the day that God created man, in the likeness of God, made
He him male and female, created He them, blessed them, and called
their name Adam.

*Maja is startled at the conclusion. The Parrot's soul brings a mask towards
Maja. He forces it on her face: It is a mask identical with "The Rape" of
Magritte.*

PARROT'S SOUL: 'Si dans le coït vous avez obtenu de glousser la glotte
et de gargouiller en même temps du pharynx et de l'anus. Cela
s'appelle faire son beurre et trier son propre persil'*

Maja groans.

ADAM: And it came to pass, when I, Adam, had lived an hundred and
thirty years, that I begat, I begat – a son!

*Out of his purse Adam pulls a little baby boy with a bowler on his head. Adam
lifts his son against the blue sky behind him and admires him.*

A son in my own likeness, after my image. As like as two peas in a
pod! I called him Seth. And the first word Seth uttered was –

Small voice from the big bowler:

Daddy!

ADAM: And Seth lived a hundred and five years and we begat –

*Now a baby boy with a bowler is delivered through a hole in the top of the big
bowler in front of Adam.*

ADAM: A son!

Adam lifts proudly his grandson in his palm against the blue sky.

ADAM: A boy in the likeness and after the image of his father and
grandfather. As like as peas in a pod. We called him Enos.

Meanwhile Seth sits on top of the big bowler.

ADAM: My son Seth lived long after that. All his days were nine hundred and twelve years. Then he passed over.

Adam throws Seth with an elegant gesture into the blue sky.

---

* (Antonin Artaud: 'van Gogh, le suicidé de la société').

ADAM: And Enos lived ninety years, and at that moment we begat –, we begat –

A new baby boy with a bowler on his babyhead comes up.

ADAM: A son! In the likeness, after the image, of his father, his grandfather and his great-grandfather. As like as peas in a pod. We called him Cainan. Then Enos passed over.

Adam throws Enos into the blue sky. Now the births and deaths are accelerated. Adam gets more and more absorbed in his offspring. He winds up the baby boys and they parade at the top of the big bowler. New baby boys appears.

My greatgrandson Cainan begat Mahalaleel, and we are all like peas in a pod. And Mahalaleel begat Jared, and Jared begat Hanok, and Hanok begat a son who was thus the son of my grandson's grandson's grandson, in my likeness, after my image. We called him Methuselah. And he begat a son who was my grandson's grandson's grandson's grandson in the likeness after the image of me and all the other great peas in our pod. We called him Lamech. And all the days of his father Methuselah, who lived in honour and glory were nine hundred sixty and nine years. Then Lamech –

Now Adam throws all his offspring into the WC. Only Lamech is left on top of the big bowler.

ADAM: Poor Lamech begat a son in pain and tears – Noah!

A naked finger comes up from within the big bowler.

ADAM: Look! That one is not at all in my own likeness!
THE FINGER: Mother!

At the word Mother Maja struggles with the mask, flings it off, stands up and looks at Noah.

ADAM: Noah, don't look at her. Look at me!

Adam forces a small bowler on the top of the finger, i.e. Noah's head.

ADAM: You shall look like me, your great ancestor!
MAJA: Look at me, Noah. I am a mother. Do give Noah to me.
ADAM: Never. I'll teach him.

With the palm of his hand Adam forces Noah, the finger, down into the big black bowler.

MAJA: You stupid man!
ADAM: Out of my sight!
MAJA: I am a mother. I am the one who gives birth.

ADAM: Sheer superstition!

MAJA: I am the Creator. And I can see that the wickedness of yours is great and that your thoughts are wicked. Beware! I will destroy you and the likes of you!

Adam shrinks away and disappears. Maja has mounted the stairs. The Parrot's soul enters the scene and balances on its edge.

PARROT'S SOUL: Yes, look at me! She has totally destroyed me.
I'm so light, all soul.

It is getting very dark. The Parrot's soul sits on the WC. Playing the accordion. Maja pours water into a little child's bucket.

MAJA: On this very day the windows of heaven will open and the rain will pour down unceasingly. And this will bring a flood of waters upon the earth to destroy everything.

Meanwhile the big bowler turns slowly, as by magic, until its brim is upwards. Now it has changed into Noah's ark.

V

The bowler's brim now upwards in the middle of the bachelor's flat.

The Parrot's soul crawls on the floor playing his flute.

PARROT'S SOUL: In the bad taste of my own time I'm going further than anyone else; at least I'm doing my best.*

Maja, inside the frame, looks at the ark (a small black bowler) on the waves of her wedding gown.

MAJA: As far as the eye can reach – Water. But lo! A tiny nutshell upon the endless ocean! And all the life is there inside.

PARROT'S SOUL: "Dans un monde où on mange chaque jour du vagin cuit avec une sauce verte" as my friend Antonin Artaud said.

MAJA: And the debt of the State increased and so did the taxes, and the End of the World was near. But in the seventh month on the seventeenth day of the month, Noah's Ark struck Mount Ararat.

Maja places the ark (the small black bowler) on top of her white belly.

---

* (André Breton).

MAJA: This is the day. My brand new man will come into being. Fresh as a daisy.

Maja peeps out of the frame into the bachelor's flat where the big black bowler (brim upward) is situated.

MAJA: Noah! Everything is new, as on the first day of Creation. I'm ready. Come, make love to me.

A phone rings inside the big bowler. The head of a young man with a bowler appears. He holds a mobile phone at his ear.

THE MAN: Hello... Yes, send it over to me. The girls can fix it for you, I promise. I'll see to it.

MAJA: That man does not even notice me!

   This must be a hallucination. Who is he? Adam?

PARROT'S SOUL: Not Adam, but the most recent great-grandson of Adam – Modern Man!

The Parrot's soul invites the modern man to a dance. The modern man now wears the big black bowler, exactly as in the beginning when the bowler appeared on two legs. They dance a joyous dance and finally the big bowler walks out the same way as he entered.

The Parrot's soul plays the saxophone. At this sound the staircase in the bachelor's flat begins to move. The staircase stops right under the frame where Maja is situated. Maja climbs slowly down the staircase into the flat. Then the Parrot's soul climbs up and leaves the earth – head upside down in the frame.

PARROT'S SOUL: 'Le merveilleux est toujours beau, n'importe quel merveilleux est beau, il n'y a même que le merveilleux qui soit beau'.*

The Parrot's soul disappears altogether.

Maja finds the baby-doll in pieces. She begins again to fit the pieces together. Now the flat has a door. It was hidden away by the staircase. Suddenly the door opens and Max peeps in.

MAX: Coffee!

MAJA: Where have you been all night!

Maja startles at her own words.

Max has prepared a tray with coffee for two.

---

* (A. Breton).

MAX: Can you imagine? I fell asleep. I slept like a log on the kitchen floor.

MAJA: What a night – an unbelievable, magical night.

MAX: My love, you look magnificent with your belly à la Mont Blanc.

MAJA: No, it's not Mont Blanc, it is Mount Ararat.

MAX: Why?

MAJA: Why? I have spent the whole night with Adam, Noah and the Modern Man.

MAX: Whom did you say you spend the night with?
Do tell me who?

MAJA: No! We shan't play that old game again!

They cuddle together while the old gramophone plays the same tune over and over again.
A hand with a green glove enters the frame, walking on two fingers. A small bowler is floating above. It might be the Parrot's soul in a new shape.

PARROT'S SOUL: (*Commenting on the lovers*) Like two parrots in a pod!
Like two parrots in a pod!

THE END

Contemporary Theatre Review
1999, Vol. 10, Part 1, pp. 57–58
Reprints available directly from the publisher
Photocopying permitted by license only

Sitting Astride Live Theatre and Animation

Johanna Enckell
Translated by Marion Baraitser

My choice is to sit astride several cultures and several disciplines. But what today has become my privilege was one time ordered by constraint. Because of the war and circumstances after the war, in my childhood I was trailed between countries and regions with very different languages, cultures and codes of conduct. Anguish before the unknown prevailed. Yet today, I cannot proceed without a dose of the unknown.

I lectured at university in the 60s and 70s on structuralism and it is this force that, little by little, gave substance and method to my discipline. But that is not the reason why these theories inform my practical theatre activities now. I always call up Roland Barthes' writings which explain how the new in art arises from new combinations and 'bricolage'. In my inner workshop there are all sorts of odds and ends to combine, little ends that become whole worlds, each separate from the other.

It is 20 years since I left the world of the university to throw myself into the practical world of the theatre, carrying my baggage of structuralism and my love of surrealism. None of this adapted to the theatrical life of Finland in the 70s. In Finland, realism was always the supreme literary and theatrical form, probably because Finnish culture awoke towards the end of the nineteenth century when realism held sway. In theatre, realism was reinforced by Stanislavski's methods, by the American theatre of Arthur Miller *et al.*, and by the impact of Brecht. Finnish theatre never knew the great ruptures of surrealism and absurdism. I found no way of implementing my preferences in the theatre there.

After 4 years as dramaturge at the Swedish theatre at Helsinki, I left for the puppet theatre of Michael Meschke in Stockholm, Sweden. Suddenly, I found myself in an atmosphere nourished by a theatre language familiar to me, where Antonin Artaud was understood and *Ubu Roi* played triumphantly with Michael Meschke. I began to write for puppet theatre which seemed to me a more free expression than writing for actors. With Gösta Kjellin (also influenced by Michael Meschke) I finished my puppet pieces for children and adults – *Noah's Hat, Mother Blue* and others. I also wrote for actors' theatre, but directors tended to radically suppress the puppet section of a piece. This finally pushed me into making my own productions. However there were two directors who completely understood my combination of actors and animation – Eric Bass, an artist much appreciated by puppeteers, and Anita Blom, actress and director. Each did a very different production of my *Dangerous Games of Saint Bridget*.

Live theatre and the theatre of animation have opposite rules. For puppeteers, technical exactitude is primordial – as exacting as manipulation and body movement. I do not wish to suggest that the actor's work is not exacting, but the way to get there is not the same. As far as the gestural is concerned, the puppeteer/actor becomes like the mimeur, who knows from the start how a timid or a rich person walks. An actor's work is often a long, interior process, secret and complicated. Everything there is tentative and uncertain. I like Peter Brook's idea, a propos of the English title of Stanislavski's *Building a Character*. This translation appears to want to say that one can build a character in the same way as one builds a wall – stone by stone. And when one has placed the last stone, the wall is finished. But Brook writes that it is not at all like that. It is more like preparing to launch a missile. One patiently prepares and polishes it, and then one day, the missile is ready to take off. But one does not know exactly when that will happen. Often the actor does not arrive at his/her launching point until well after the premiere.

If the puppeteer does not always understand the actor's methods, actors are often full of admiration for the scrupulous work of puppeteers. This is understandable. Actors have generally come across puppets, but not professionally, so theatre directors let them work it out for themselves. When Eric Bass or Jean-Claude Leportier give demonstrations to theatre actors, their attention is intense.

It is only during this last year, 20 years after my debut in the theatre, that I feel I have attained my interior world, with all its theories, philosophies, paintings, dreams and experiences that searched so long for a means of expression. This occurred in a little surrealist comedy lasting 45 minutes – *Nuptial Night*. I put it on at Teatteri Mukamas, a small theatre in the town of Tampere. I worked with three bright, young and curious actors. In rehearsals, I replaced puppets with the hands of the actors, and used objects suggesting surreal places. Together we studied surrealist texts and for guidance we chose Andre Breton's text: 'The marvellous is always beautiful – No matter what marvel is beautiful, it is only the marvellous that can be beautiful.'

In Puck No 8, review of the International Institut of Puppetry in Charleville – Mézières.

The Head or Watch it, Kid!

Dennis Silk

In Memory of Louis

Contemporary Theatre Review
1999, Vol. 10, Part 1, pp. 61–69
Reprints available directly from the publisher
Photocopying permitted by license only

The Head or Watch it, Kid!

PERSONS

High-chair baby
Young Lady
Her admirer
Her mother
Her mother's admirer
Headsman
Head

The backcloth is painted jig-saw style. Across its top, in schoolboy block letters:

Jig-Saw Theatre First Time Ever

Its central figure goes back to the Pierrot cut-outs published by Epinal. But instead of the traditional Pierrot costume and trunk and lopped-off limbs, a commuter of René Magritte smiles dismembered there: bland face completed by bowler-hat; trunk distinctly separated from its head but with well-disposed civic tie and collar, and jacket faintly indicated under overcoat; two languishing trouser-legs, one to left, one to right, of trunk; shoes heraldic under trunk. Disposed around this cut-out: knife, fork, spoon, plate, tumbler, salt-cellar, also in the plain Magritte manner.

THE YOUNG LADY MARIONETTE is roly-poly as a fattest Matrioshka doll. She is three to four feet high.
HER MOTHER MARIONETTE is tall and thin as a totem. She and her daughter are highly rouged, with piled-up Fuseli hair-dos.
THE TWO ADMIRERS One wide-shouldered, thick-necked, the other narrow-shouldered, thin-necked.
HIGH-CHAIR BABY Preferably a real baby but generous about lolly-pops. Some of the time plays with a yo-yo. Somewhat monstrous in his pink high-chair and red, white and blue pinafore.

THE HEAD is impaled on a pike placed in a gocart pushed around by the headsman. (Or it could be worn as a mask by an actor whose body suggests a pike.) Its voice is off-stage. Eyes and mouth can be manipulated to open or close. The mouth should not slavishly represent the shape of the off-stage syllables. It should represent them in a stylised way.

HEADSMAN Should suggest weak ferocity. A toy axe hangs from a gold belt around his contemporary dinner-jacket.

TRUNK A dignified tailor's dummy, rather shabby, on a baluster-like support. It is not seen till the headsman has almost completed shaving the head.

The two ladies, their admirers and the high-chair baby watch the action from somewhat raised positions, or else from a roped-off perimeter. It's a public ceremony, or its aftermath.

HEAD: Please put me together again.

HEADSMAN: You're asking 2 plus 2 to make 5.

HEAD: 2 plus 2 do make 5.

HEADSMAN: You confuse me.

HEAD: *You're* confused. *I'm* ashamed. I'm in a very serious position. Cut off, so to say. And all these (*indicates ladies and admirers*) these people watching my shame. It's humbling. (*weeps*)

HEADSMAN: Use this hanky. (*takes one from young lady*) She waved it at you during that great speech you made.

HEAD: Use your head, man. You can see I can't... (*headsman blows his nose for him*)

HEADSMAN: Feeling better? Pacified?

HEAD: No, I'm not. My own voice cut off. Over there somewhere. A trunk-call. I just can't get through. (*again weeps*) I feel so itsy-bitsy. Like a ventriloquist's dummy that lost its ventriloquist.

HEADSMAN: It's very untidy here on this square. I suppose this boot here was yours. And all this   other stuff here. This bowler-hat.

HEAD: Don't upset me.

HEADSMAN: This trouser-leg. And all those   over there   those.

HEAD: Please don't.

HEADSMAN: This brief-case of important documents.

HEAD: Copy of my speech.

HEADSMAN: I didn't really catch everything you said.

HEAD: I was interrupted.

HEADSMAN: Please complete it.

HEAD: Hands.

HEADSMAN: I'll hold it up for you, you can read it.

HEAD: Citizens, you know my hatred of faction. This dear common-wealth of ours, to what can I liken it? It is one great speech with eight parts to it. There is the common noun that is the citizen the adjective that is the police-force qualifying it the verb that is the public transport system… well, I had just arrived at my peroration, the conjuction, when by the action of your blade you deprived me of my definite article.

HEADSMAN: Sorry. (*indicates daughter.*) She greatly liked all you said.

HEAD: Thank you, thank you.

HEADSMAN: You've scored a success, I would say.

HEAD: A success! I've been breakfasted on. Confiscated. Tripes and toes and trunk, I could go round the whole world looking for me. All the parts of a man. I could call out in Iceland to my trunk that's waiting patiently for me in England. I'm a much-handled property. I'll be shop-soiled before they put me together again. I imagine the trunk of me sitting in some bus now, collected, staring calmly out of the window at autumn fields. A delicious sadness, no doubt, staring out at those fields. And he has a paid ticket for a long journey across America, and supposes he will keep company with himself forever.

(*The ladies clap at this speech*)

They're clapping for failure. Connoisseurs of failure. They're scaffold-dolls confirming my failure. How humiliating. All these   heartless houses and dolls.   Polish your teeth, you whores.

HEADSMAN: They've a living to make like anyone else. Why can't you be nice to them? You've got a lot of time to spend here under their window, observed by them. And they've got a lot of waiting to do. So why not be nice to one another?

HEAD: So tedious, so tedious. They help rouge in all this whiteness I feel here, whiteness instead of sweetness. Maybe I'll do what you say. You there. Madam, up there, queen of this stinking alley, you have a charming daughter.

MOTHER: Thank you.

HEAD: And you, young lady, you have a charming protectress to intervene for you in every moral issue.

DAUGHTER: Thank you.

HEAD: I may look perhaps a little poverty-struck, but here, in this brief-case this kind gentleman indicates to you now, I have a considerable sum. If you were to descend your stew-smelly stairs…

(*She does*)

DAUGHTER: Twenty dollars.

HEAD: This gentleman will make them over to you immediately.

DAUGHTER: Short-time.

HEAD: This gentleman will make over another twenty dollars.
DAUGHTER: All right.

(*The young lady removes head from its pike and places it behind a door she opens in herself. She then closes the door. She starts a pendulum movement of her head and shoulders, at the same time declaiming "Tick tock tick tock more more tick tock tick more more tick tock tick tick tick."*)

HEAD (*inside young lady*): Oh mummy. It's nice here … pink bedroom walls, a victrola, I can hear a mouse-trap snapping in the corner. Oops. There goes another mouse. Watch it, kid!

(*Victrola music:* "Oh grant me a home / Where the buffalo roam / Where the deer and the antelope play.")
(*The young lady removes head from its home and replaces it on the pike.*)

HEADSMAN: How was it?
HEAD: Temporary.
HEADSMAN: Try again maybe.
HEAD: I wish I knew how to shrug.
HEADSMAN: We will try again. (*addresses the wide-shouldered admirer*) My dear sir, I wonder whether you would concede this gentleman a space on your shoulder. The world owes him much. I, too, owe him amends for a sharp injustice done him. I know you present a handsome front to the world but I personally consider you would look better two-headed. Let me try you for size.

(*He succeeds in his temporary placement of the head but wide-shoulders shrugs him off quickly to be caught by the headsman.*)

ADMIRER: Squatter.
HEAD: Aboriginal.
HEADSMAN: Self-sufficient wretch. Time will show you your lack of Siamese sense.

(*addresses narrow shoulders*)

Sir, I think you will do better without your head. May I suggest this replacement? Think what it will do for you to have a good head on your shoulders at last. (*He performs this substitution. The new head falls off every time he replaces it. He doesn't know what to do with the former one. He tries it out on the pike but it doesn't fit. He juggles with heads, gets confused, in trying to catch his own head drops the two others. The pike-head lies on the floor. "Watch it, kid!", from off-stage. He picks up both heads, dusts them, puts them back on the right pike or shoulders. Clatter-bone music to all this.*)

HEAD: Phew! (*headsman wipes sweat off his brow for him*) Thank you.
HEADSMAN: We have one last address.
HEAD: Who?
HEADSMAN: The mother. (*Addresses her*)
Madam, your daughter is mistress of such temporary arrangements. Perhaps you could more permanently dispose of my friend's head.
MOTHER: He is a permanent paying-guest?
HEADSMAN: There is also money, much money.
MOTHER: I have kept a place in my heart for him.

(*The headsman removes the mother's head, neck and trunk, inserts the pike-head above her thighs, replaces her missing parts. The head stares out from between her trunk and thighs, a little perplexed.*)

HEADSMAN: No, this doesn't seem the right landscape either. How does it feel down there?
HEAD: I don't like this mummy, either. She's voluminous.

(*Exasperated headsman rescues the head from its involvement, settles account with the mother in dumb-show.*)

HEAD: I'm back where I started. A head here in the sun. A small boulder with a big memory. I've been *rebuffed*. I don't belong to the tribe of heads any more. I'm that nuisance, a country-cousin.
Some heads have big town-mansions to live in. I've known whole families of well-connected heads. No one shrugged them off. Elegant, so elegant. And worldly. My, all those mirrors, that glass.
It's insupportable. I think I'll sleep it off.
HEADSMAN: You're going to sleep?
HEAD: If I can.
HEADSMAN: Well, good night.
HEAD: Good night. Maybe good-bye.
HEADSMAN: What do you mean?
HEAD: Maybe if I shut my eyes, I'll wish you away. Maybe it's really not true I mean
HEADSMAN: Pardon?
HEAD: The blade and all that. Please forgive me.
HEADSMAN: Finish what you have to say.
HEAD: I mean maybe it's not true. That basket over there into which I rolled, maybe it's all just my wicked dream. (*closes eyes*)
HEADSMAN: You'd better decide about that when you wake up. (*to ladies above*) He thinks it's a wicked dream. That's insulting. (*to head*) I'm insulted.
HEAD: (*opens its eyes*): I beg your pardon.
HEADSMAN: You insulted me.

HEAD: I've just done my best to doze off. It's difficult to insult anyone when you're dozing off.

HEADSMAN: You thought I was a bad dream you could do away with.

HEAD: And I was having such a good dream. Then you hack your way into it.

HEADSMAN: Oh, what were you dreaming about?

HEAD: In this dream a handsome shabby beggar entered a tailor's, a small tailor, in a side-street. Do you have any cast-offs for me? he asked. Anything my size? The tailor being a charitable man took him up to his loft where all kinds of things were lying around – old forgotten sewing machines, old bales of unfashionable material, old sawdusty dummies. Among these old things, these Factory Acts from a long time back, there was one particular large package …

HEADSMAN: You interest me greatly.

HEAD: This package interested the beggar also. He asked the tailor to open it. The tailor, who was himself puzzled and wanted to know the contents of this package …

HEADSMAN: Please continue.

HEAD: As he was about to untie the last string, you woke me.

HEADSMAN: That would have been an interesting dream.

HEAD: It was an interesting dream. It's made me thirsty.

HEADSMAN: Perhaps you would like to drink something?

HEAD: Some water. This dream   these houses   they parch me.

(*The baby passes down a glass of water to the headsman. He offers it to the head to drink from.*)

HEAD: Thank you. You know, you may not believe it but …

HEADSMAN: Yes?

HEAD: Suddenly I'm very hungry.

(*Baby hands down lollipop*)

HEAD: Thank you but it will spoil my appetite.

HEADSMAN: You're thinking about your stomach again.

HEAD: Eggs. Poached, fried, scrambled and boiled. Sausages. Coiling strings of sausages.

HEADSMAN (*To ladies above*): His memory serves him up sausages.

HEAD: Salt cellars. Serviettes. The laid table.

HEADSMAN: (*to ladies above*): He lays the table.

HEAD: Waiter. I say, waiter, there.

HEADSMAN: I clap my hands for him.

HEAD: I want service at this table. Service, I say.

HEADSMAN: Yes, sir, can I take your order, sir?

HEAD: Sausages, I wanted. And eggs, poached. Haven't I seen you somewhere before, waiter?

HEADSMAN: It may be I served you somewhere before, sir.

HEAD: You never pleased me. You don't provide even the basic tools.

HEADSMAN: Tools, sir?

HEAD: Cutlery, where's the cutlery?

(*Headsman-waiter claps hands, baby hands him down knife, fork and plate. Voice off-stage:* Kniiife Fooork Plaaate Sauuusages Eegs. *Head symbolically eats a sausage.*)

HEAD: Whisk them away for me, James.

HEADSMAN: What, sir?

HEAD: All these   these flies. Blood fascinates. Get rid of them, James.

(*Headsman runs around stage, flapping away at flies.*)

HEADSMAN: Enjoy the meal, sir?

HEAD: Not really, James. I need a tube of toothpaste to sweeten my imagination.

HEADSMAN: Perhaps you really need a shave, sir. Shaving rejuvenates.

HEAD: I imagine I can feel my stubble, James. A two-day growth, I should imagine. You check for me, James.

HEADSMAN: I can feel your stubble all right, sir.

HEAD: What I need is a shave, don't you think, James?

HEADSMAN: I would say a shave is called for, sir.

(*He brings in shaving tackle and mirror, and begins to shave the head. Holds up mirror for head to see shave.*)

HEAD: A bit more under the chin, James.

HEADSMAN: That better, sir?

HEAD: You've rejuvenated me. James, you're a good fellow. Maybe I'll be able to see the day through.   James, over there, at the side of the mirror…

HEADSMAN: Yes, sir.

HEAD: … something's given me quite a start.

HEADSMAN: In the mirror, sir?

HEAD: Reflected in the mirror. Now I've cut myself.

HEADSMAN: (*peering into mirror*): I don't see anything at all.

(*Light focuses on tailor's dummy, representing trunk of unhoused head. It is kneeling at the block.*)

HEAD: But I do.   James, you know what that is?

HEADSMAN: I don't exactly recall, sir.

HEAD: That's my trunk. I thought it was travelling across America.

HEADSMAN: Now you say so, sir, it does look remarkably like a trunk.

HEAD: I didn't think to see it again. You can congratulate me.

HEADSMAN: I do congratulate you, sir.

HEAD: You think   he's praying, James? He looks so serious.

HEADSMAN: In this half-light, sir, you could conceive that.

HEAD: A soldier waiting patiently for orders. I feel like (*indicating baby's yo-yo*)   like that yo-yo, always in motion, when I look at him.

HEADSMAN: I like best its muteness.

HEAD: Muteness! Probably he's listening hard to himself. Probably he's working things out down there. I feel flighty   so flighty.

HEADSMAN: A man should never reproach himself.

HEAD: I did him little good. (*weeps*)

HEADSMAN: Please pull yourself together.

HEAD: He seems so   exposed there. Perhaps you could dress him again.

HEADSMAN: Isn't that going a little far?

HEAD: Public morals.

HEADSMAN: Ah!

HEAD: This boot here. And all those   over there   those

HEADSMAN: You're so dressy.
>Ladies and gentlemen, now we dress the patient animal.
>This well-laced boot... (*flourishes it*)

HEAD: It would be easier to dress him if you stood him up.

HEADSMAN: You shine today. (*stands trunk up*)
>... chaste trouser
>sage shirt (*dresses trunk in shirt*)
>Ladies and gentlemen, a dead man's wardrobe.
>One entire identi-kit.

LADIES: Lovely, lovely.

HEAD: You forgot the hat.

HEADSMAN: (*picks up hat*) One religious hat.
>Can this hat live?
>(*tries it out, unsuccessfully, on trunk*)
>We're going to need a hat-rack.

HEAD: Try me. I could fit so   snug.

HEADSMAN: (*mockingly*) I know a hat you've been attached to a long time.

HEAD: Please put me together again.

HEADSMAN: I know a hat that's been languishing for you a long time.

HEAD: Me and my trunk and my hat took a walk in the park. Just the three of us, garlanded with green. No one rouged in that park, no listeners at windows. Mr. Three, I said to my trunk, tell us about your travels. Then Mr. Two (that's my hat) will dance us a horn-pipe.

HEADSMAN: Sounds cramped with the three of you.

HEAD: It was a big park.

HEADSMAN: Three in one stuffy room. Stealing one another's oxygen.

HEAD: Mr. Three, I said to my trunk, will you teach me to map-read?

(Light begins slowly to fade on tailor's dummy.)

HEADSMAN: I don't think he'll have the time for that.
Mr. Three, say something.

HEAD: Mr. Three, you're going away again? Travelling across America? Laughing in some sleeping-car about me?

HEADSMAN: Mr. Three is going away. *(laughs)*

HEAD: Mr. Three, you can lie on some sidewalk and die.

HEADSMAN: Mr. Three is very high in himself.

HEAD: I can't see him any more. Mr. Three, you're absconding.

HEADSMAN: All I can see is a bowler-hat going away.

HEAD: It's my wardrobe you're going off in. Mr. Three, I'll tell them about you in America.

HEADSMAN: The kids on the sidewalk are bowing to Mr. Three. He looks grand. Mr. Three has got a million dollars.

HEAD: Mr. Three must be thinking about me in America. He looks at himself in a mirror. Touches himself gingerly. Careful, he says, gingerly. Don't press too hard. Everything is carefully thought-out, weighed. Mr. Three doesn't need even one pillow. He could sleep on the sidewalk. Or a block. Mr. Three is touching that place where a head should be. A long thought from America.

First published by The Sheep Meadow Press, Riverdale-on-Hudson, New York, in *William The Wonder-Kid: Plays, Puppet Plays and Theater Writings*. © 1996 Dennis Silk. All rights reserved.

The Marionette Theatre

Dennis Silk

Contemporary Theatre Review
1999, Vol. 10, Part 1, pp. 73–83
Reprints available directly from the publisher
Photocopying permitted by license only

The Marionette Theatre

Part One

"Shutters shut and open. So do queens."

Gertrude Stein

I

A Japanese traveller, Saikaku, has a tricky story about umbrellas. Twenty of them hung outside the temple at Kwannon. People borrowed them in bad weather. In spring 1649, an unlucky umbrella-borrower had it blown out of his hand by a divine wind. Travelling further maybe than Saikaku, the umbrella landed at the village of Amazato. No one there had seen an umbrella. But from its ribs, numbering forty, and the unusual luminosity of its oil-paper, they knew the sun-god had landed at Amazato. They built a shrine to the umbrella.

Saikaku does not describe the landing of the umbrella. But it must descend slowly on Amazato from *up there*, slowly and in considered spirals as a god should. After the vigorous theophany of its descent, it lies stranded in the market-square. Yet everyone understands the umbrella is latent. A farmer closes his fingers around its handle as around a staff-hook. They travel gingerly up the limb of this god, they feel a metal obstruction then a yielding. The umbrella shuts. *Deus absconditus*. But what shuts opens, like fingers. Open shut. This farmer becomes the attendant of the opening and shutting god.

II

The umbrella teases. It opens. Then folds back on itself. Really, it's two umbrellas. Yet it's one. A villager would have to have two minds to grasp this. Moreover, its mode of arrival draws attention to itself. So they build a shrine to it. Best to abandon it to mystery. Amazato bundles away the umbrella in a shrine.

And it's a jealous god. There is no god but the umbrella. That's because Amazato doesn't pay attention. In the street outside, the small red spinning top has been hoarding its conversation a long time. Gathering itself together for a definitive statement. Speech after long silence. And its cousin, the yo-yo, opens and shuts shop. Here is the eight-year-old shopkeeper. His balloon declared itself at half-past nine this morning. Then went into tininess. The god sulks.

The umbrella should make a place for them in the shrine. It should hold a nest of gods. Umbrella, yo-yo, spinning top, balloon. A cotton-reel. And a frontiers man to play a concertina for the gods. Breath sucked in and out. Now we're leaving Amazato. We're high as an umbrella. This flag over the shrine waits. Waits for a lucky wind to give it life. Unfolds and flaps in the wind.

III

The queer pendulum life ferries us there, and back. *There* is the seed-life. (Or of dead grain.) *Here* is here. The two-fold tribe are performers, they perform their two lives. They're like an actor waiting to go on, so half-way perhaps between two lives he could scarcely tell you who he is. The life of the flag above the shrine is also two-fold. First, stiff, folded back on itself, then declaring itself for movement. But the flag is performed rather than a performer. And a bale of cloth is performed in the street. This street-salesman unfolds an arm's-length of it, then teasingly folds it back on itself. Again a mystery. But the cloth itself scarcely performs.

The same for this regiment of tin soldiers preparing for war. They're the played rather than the players. And of this marble wanting to be flicked. What's this needle doing? There and back. There and back. The seamstress hides her thinking under her eyelids. Pins and needles – seamstresses' cathedrals.

Needles are used rather than performed. Or unused. Till someone makes much of them. They too are in the folded and unfolding life. Like this savage tribe of the kitchen. It screams in the drawer, or on the shelf, it demands conscription. Here are the drones, or proles, of this tribe: cheese-grater, potato-peeler, corkscrew, pestle, rolling-pin, cake-pattern, coffee-mill. Here's the managerial class: knife, fork, spoon, plate, cup, glass. They all belong to the *rending* tribe, the tribe of tooth. They're at continual war with the seamstress in her *remembering* room: the life in things is put together there, patched up, reconstituted. It's in alliance with certain lives in the children's playroom next door: scattered pieces of jig-saw remembering the original puzzle, building bricks planning a town, alphabet blocks working out language. What are we to say about the seamstress? She remembers, retrieves. Yet her molars aren't there for nothing.

IV

We say *animism*. Then we put it back on the shelf with the other relegated religions. Maybe our flight from animism is our flight from madness. We're afraid of the life we're meagre enough to term inanimate. Meagre because we can't cope with those witnesses. Rainer Maria Rilke hesitates whether to abandon a bar of soap in a hotel-room. During Gilles de Rais' confession, the Bishop of Nantes covers the Cross. (The world of wood, incarnate in the Cross, rejects Gilles.) If a cross is a witness, why not a loaf of bread, or a shoe-tree, or a sugar-tongs, or a piece of string? We should have an All Souls' Night for dead objects, and confer on them some hours of the life we deny them.

V

His heavy, dangling life marks out what's possible. Whatever came out of lumpishness to dance to us. It's the marionette from Lyon, the trans-formation dancer. Incorporating coffins, and chairs, and tables. A coat-hanger. A hat rack. Needle and thread. Dancing for them to us. It's All Souls' Night. Dancing in a muck-sweat. Two-fold life's thick in this man. He marks out his tiny patch. Fights for three feet of life. He dances for the sake of a pair of shoe-laces, for a bereaved hat. Privileged ghostly spectators cram the stage. Caskets and cupboards. A commode on its last legs. They're like a group of one-legged men watching a good dancer. They have their best chance in him.

The unexpected charge of all these souls fuses the lights. Lights Lights we shout. The man from Lyon stands there striking matches. Lighting up possibility. Terror! A struck match.

VI

The marionette salaams to us, shuts his eyes. A mahogany wardrobe observes his trance-strong face. He's propped up in a corner. He's in *samadhi*. Travelling for everyone.

The marionette, in *samadhi*, controls the audience by the strength of his will. It's like a commode with locked drawers that fascinate us.

He hasn't fluffed his exit or muffed his lines. (Unlike the spinning top.) He's more tricks up his sleeve than an umbrella. Now he's in the folded life. But he could lash out and scare everyone.

Part Two

"King Charles walked and talked an hour after his head was cut off."

I

The marionette is a poet from Peru who got education. He comes from a long way off to talk to us. He talks of bread and trousers and the crease in a shirt. Because he is safe among things, because he is himself a thing, a "thing thing", he allows himself our town-talk. He kneels to talk to dismembered man.

He doesn't have the impediments of an actor. An actor's body is so untalented. It doesn't have doors, it doesn't take in pain, it can't play us the world-tooth rending and shredding. It merely walks and talks around that tooth. The marionette – because it is a thing and yet a man – because it is this poet from Peru – plays us this mastication of things, and of ourselves. The marionette is shredded over the suburbs. He plays us the world-breakfast. His well-jointed body speaks for us. He uses the nearest grammar to hand. "I simply couldn't contain myself", he says. And comes apart at the joints. "Pull yourself together", he's admonished. His scattered parts do their best to come together. "I couldn't keep my eyes off her", he confesses. She removes his eyes with distaste from her private parts.

He's an accurate grammarian. He's devoured and disgorged. He contracts and expands. He does acts of nut-cracker cruelty, expiates them with his own head, plucks out his eye for a woman, performs Caesareans, swells to the balloon he flies off in, opens like a Queen-for-One-Night-Only, shuts like Venus-Fly-Trap. His head observes its trunk making off down a side-street. He's a man about town, a man about town on his last legs. His head sings the complete man: buttocks and toes and fingers and eyes, that reconstituted man he thought about in Peru. "I'll be very changed", he says, "before I'm changed."

II

Mother fork, grandmother fork, ex-father fork, the child says, laying the cutlery out on the playroom floor. (Tooth and memory, two machines working against each other.) The head of the stacking toy lies on the playroom floor. All you can see is the back of this head. He seems to be inquiring deeply of a tile. His dismantled parts call out Help from the battlefield. Heroes have come apart at the joints. They ask to get kitted out again. This deficiency can tell against them in the long run.

The head starts travelling across the floor. Probably he's looking for a way back. Probably the other parts of this dismembered man are craning their necks to find the legal instrument. (After all, a head does have juris-diction over his parts.) His yellow throat must be craning its neck, his red trunk – in the corner over there – must be craning its neck, all the *disjecta membra* of this man's body must be remembering him. Blocks of wood thinking about the original tree.

In the meantime, the head's travelling. He confronts the camp of the enemy. Fatigues and drill. Everything you think of when you say Khaki. But the head soldiers on. He travels this playroom floor the entire day looking for the parts of a man. Saluting meccano. Attending parades for a foundered horse. He could spend a day and a playroom night inspect-ing this floor. And nothing accomplished.

The head is a foot-soldier sent out to foreign parts. Made use of by Empire. He knows he is a head but no longer knows what a head is. Everything's so topsy-turvy on a battle-field. (His trunk just tried to get a message through to him but was outflanked by the cavalry.) And say he found his trunk, here, on this battlefield blurred in jig-saw, what would happen? He could think his trunk his head, or his head his trunk. Now he remembers what a hand is but no longer remembers its name. It's lucky he remembers fingers are gloved in shoes. He could think his great left toe his big right thumb if he hadn't remembered his right ankle is his left wrist. Now that boy-soldier from Hong-Kong has banged his drum into his head. Is it? Say his head is his head, his trunk his trunk. What's next? Say he slips his trunk on right, he'll screw the head on back to front. Such junketings!

III

Index finger says Yes. But it's Thumb's down, anyway. Small finger says Maybe. Big brother middle finger says Calm down, everyone. Number Four says All right.

Right hand sugar. Left hand salt.
Molars grind. Heart says Sorry.
He put his best foot forward. His worst foot went to sleep.

***

He redeems his promissory notes to the world-bank with toes and fingers, buttocks and eyes. His bereaved trousers limp off to the bank to redeem the last note.

***

A Caesarean performed on a hearty-eater marionette. Out comes a baby marionette clutching a butcher's bill: 1 lb. lamb chops
3 lb. salt beef
Whose intestines?

A waiter interviews this new arrival: Is that an Indian scripture you have there, sir? (*Indicating butcher's bill*.) A saving gospel from up there? (*Indicating sky*.)

The new-born puppet begins greedily to steal from the hearty eater's plate. (*Who withdrawing his plate appeals to the waiter*.) Let me keep my meat in your safe. (*He opens the waiter, hides the meat in his insides*.)

***

Opening the door in his head he takes out his still-born child.
Closing the door in his chest he hides his still-born child.
To-day, he says, I feel the whole world is a door.

***

Fingers skilfully, restlessly, empty pockets. Their master directs them from bed. (This pickpocket never travels to work with his body because he's afraid of being identified.)

***

The day before her wedding she visits the dressmaker. Forget about that wedding-dress, she says. I'm betrothed to a headless groom. Have you the sewing machine that will put him together again?

***

At the doll-hospital: two old ladies insert the stuffing in dolls, their hair, their eyes.

IV

Cut-Out

a

Your head won't need its hat any more. It lies here oddly intact without its trunk. Was it some Judith who cut it off? Your arms like dolphins fly about their business. Your feet stand in their pumps at the Coroner's. Someone has made a cut-out of all your parts.

b

Won't you join the dance? I won't, you say, no I can't. I don't have a breath long enough. I've the left lung of a suicide, it refuses to breathe in. What's that musician trying to do? My left leg keeps Greenwich Time, my right's gone to sleep in New York. Is that a wedding-march he's try-ing to strike up? But my ring-finger's divorced its hand. My hat's an affront to this street. Merely tooth marries air. Greedyguts, saying All right. (But it is not right not to publish these banns.)

c

A whistle blows. Someone is directing the traffic. For the wedding, in the next street, of dismembered man. Careful, you say, gingerly. I can scarcely pull myself together, scarcely stand up. With a somewhat sheepish smile you ransack your memory. Send your leg down looking for your ankle. A scouting party to look for your wrist. Eight then ten fin-gers. Ditto toes. Two or so eyes. (They are not glass.) You're kitted out. Tear-ducts and memory. You put your best foot forward. You're a man of parts.

Part Three

"We're in the sleeping life. A hundred strings play the dream."

A. Tryphon

I

It's the Fantoccini man, the master of the marionettes. Sitting down, in the nineteenth century, to his fowl and wine. He wears a frock-coat but-toned at the waist, a high black stock, turkey-grease runs down the entire length of his shirt front. He's dining out on the takings. Bones on his plate remind him of his come-apart marionettes. He worked them, to-night, in "the very first of drawing rooms". A menu of marionettes for the London aristocrats. But he's stolen the royalty from his marionettes. These favourites of heaven came unstuck in London. They're the dream of a mechanic. He reviews his dream. *Item*: A Scaramouch with no head and afterwards all head. His neck shot up to a great man's ceiling. Ceiling not sky. The connection is with pockets. *Item*: Judy Callaghan with six figures jumping out of *her* pocket. *Item*: A Nondescript juggling with his head. First of all Somebody, afterwards Nobody. *Item*: The Parson in his Pulpit. (But an atheist among marionettes.) *Item*: The Polander balancing a chair and two poles. You'll gape spreadeagled, Polander. *Item*: A Policeman splitting down the middle. And he doesn't blow his whistle for the real theft. This Fantoccini man has stripped his puppet-shreds of all their valuables. Gutted their memory. No more sending memory down side-streets for news of themselves. They lie here like freethinkers. They're retrieved by the perfectly organized secular strings in the hard hands of this Fantoccini man. Now it's time for knife and fork. After a hard evening of snapping orders at Judy Callaghan. Fifty strings I worked for that Judy. Hot and hidden managing that bitch.

II

The dream-shreds lie scattered on the carpet. Secular children for a Victorian mansion. The Polander's fallen between two fools. The first fool is the hard fool, the Fantoccini man, with clicking heels, martial handshake, waxed look in Victorian sleep. The second fool's the soft fool, the contemporary fool. He's a teddy-bear courting a totem. Cuddling his dream now. Performing his parlour tricks, this puppeteer disowns his own marionettes. Paderewski at the piano. Christopher Robin saying his prayers. Charming assumptions have put the puppeteer to sleep. The marionette's doing his best to stay awake through all this. He begins to realize his position isn't easy. Such a soft master to make such a hard thing. And master doesn't know he has a dangerous object on his hands. He's like a sapper defusing the mines he plants. He likes the blue eyes of his marionette too much to see what they focus on. He can't follow the straight road of the marionette he's made. Actually, he doesn't want to. He likes children, he likes pillows.

III

The abused marionette appeals to us. Use me, please use me. Don't kill me in a dream. Send me out. This hand of mine could win the Punic Wars. This head of mine is the entire family of Zen Patriarchs.

The puppeteer doesn't listen. His own family's gone to sleep, his whole body's a big puppeteering yawn. He indomitably yawns.

We're sleepy, too. Sleep runs down our face, we try to wipe it out of our eyes in the morning, our foot's gone to sleep over some trying task. Lazybones.

Sleepy love-affairs. Bowing and scraping before the absent heart. That heart went out the window in sleep last night. It's playing leap-frog in the courtyard. Some other woman smiles at you.

Snoozing over tea-break and heart-break. Snoozing kid.

***

A puppeteer, waking, would study the difference between sleepers and men. Study lovers like spinning-tops, or ninepins in a bowling-alley. Nothing royal. Study their wooden luck. For the lovers are all in the lock-up, the toy-theatre.

IV

The hero of Hoffman's "The Sandman" falls in love with Olympia, who the same time every night plays the harp at her window. Later he dances with her at a ball, she never speaks to him but she's a marvellous dancer. Of course she's an automaton, a perfect doll.

Fascination of automatons, of the perfect response lost in clockwork. Had Hoffman written for the puppet-theatre, a young automaton would discover, with what horror, the clockwork in Olympia.

V

A Houdini bill from 1914:

DARING DIVE!

This Wednesday, July 15

– 12.30 P.M. sharp –
Battery, Near The Aquarium

Harry
HOUDINI

Now Appearing At Hammerstein's
Victoria Theatre and Roof Garden

Securely handcuffed and leg-ironed will be placed in a heavy pack-
ing case, which will be nailed and roped, then encircled by steel
bands, firmly nailed. Two hundred pounds of iron weights will then
be lashed to this box containing HOUDINI. The box will then be
THROWN INTO THE RIVER. Houdini will undertake to release
himself whilst submerged under water.

There's a puppet-vocabulary in Houdini: the handcuffed soul, the strait-
jacketed soul, the soul locked in a filing-cabinet at the river-bottom. The
sleepwalker down there sends up bubbles to comfort the family.

Part Four

"This is the place, gentlemen."

Abraca dabraca banana. This puppeteer, plausible mountebank, does his
spiel for the populace. He plays them his entire stock: marionettes grated
round town like cheese, or peeling themselves like that Norwegian going
into an onion. (Cold now, in late October, without a coat.) He knows the
language of coats and toes. Of four-fingered men. Of marionettes confis-
cating each other's parts. "I confiscate your right eye, Edward Grey.
You've been such a naughty boy." Marionette-orphans of broken-down
kitchens. Tripes billow from their mouth like balloons in a comic-strip.
Tripes and smiles. Cries of No more No more. A hearty-eater marionette
throws his own head to the populace. Hardy little boys throw it back
laughing. (They don't know it's serious to have a head thrown at you in
October.)

Marionettes open like umbrellas in late October. These rain-clouds are
waiting to say something. The mountebank looks up carefully at the sky.
Mounts his bench and chatters. Assistants carry out a coffin from his
booth. (Should I tell this town my secrets? he asks himself. Shouldn't I
have locked the door of that booth?) He stands there in apparent surprise. What do you have here for us? he asks these mourners. It seems
they don't know. With an effort he forces the coffin-lid. To go by his look,
it can't really be empty down there. He addresses the populace. "Ladies
and gentlemen, you don't know what it is to serve the dead. I do. I got
this grammar-book (*holding it up*) from their own mouths. That one there
(*indicating a rival puppeteer*), that one there just leafs through the dictionary.

Ladies and gentlemen, I give you Cesare the somnambulist." And raises Cesare by a primitive rod to the head. Waxen Cesare opens his eyes very slowly. From a coffin to a crowd. Looks wildly at outside. Clearly he's thinking about this and that. Now he's decided on something. Opening the door of his chest he shows, painted inside, the body of his soul. A childlook to that painting. Raising his right arm, he copies the gesture of the interior arm. "Here is the place", he says, "here".

First published by The Sheep Meadow Press, New York, in *William The Wonder-Kid: Plays, Puppet-Plays and Theater-Writings* © 1996 Dennis Silk.

Contemporary Theatre Review
1999, Vol. 10, Part 1, pp. 85–88
Reprints available directly from the publisher
Photocopying permitted by license only

Appendix A:
Questionnaire: Puppetry as a Theatrical Art

Compiled by Marion Baraitser

This questionnaire is based on the puppeteer Steve Tillis' *Towards an Aesthetic of the Puppet.*

It is of *vital importance* to the reader of the collection of modern adult puppet theatre plays that he/she understands the context of how the plays are made and how they work on stage. *Your answers to the questionnaire will greatly help this process.*

1. How do you define a puppet in theatrical performance?
2. In what theatrical context(s) do your puppets perform? Are you drawing on specific cultural traditions of making puppet theatre?
3. Do you see puppetry as a distinctive form of theatre? Would you say it has its own laws and conditions?
   Do you confront puppet theatre with live theatre so the characteristics of the puppet theatre are intensified?
4. How do you see the relationship between the puppets/objects and their 'speakers of the text'?

   (a) What would you say are the differences between the puppet as 'character,' and character in theatre?
   (b) Do you use actors as puppets?
      If so, why?
   (c) What relationship do your puppets have with the performed text?
   (d) Do you allow for a relationship between your puppets and a character outside the text?
      If so, why?
   (e) Do you want to establish a relationship between the puppets and the puppet artist?
      If so, why?

5. How do you move your puppets?

    (a) Do you use puppets that are 3-D, or flat (or both)?

    (b) Which of the following control mechanics do you use to move your puppets?:

        Hand puppets/glove puppets:

            (If you use hand puppets, do you regard hand puppets as part of the actor and of mime – or the hand as apart from the actor and therefore, an 'object'?)

        Shadow puppets:

        Rod puppets:

            controlled from above/below, or controlled with one hand moving the hinged mouth while the other hand controls rods.

        Jointed puppets (with strings or wire) controlled from above:

        Jigging puppets:

        Magnetically controlled puppets:

        Puppets controlled by three persons (as in Bunraku):

        Please describe and comment on your choice.

    (c) The relationship of the puppets to the audience taking part in the illusion created:

        Do you think that the puppet theatre's unique ability to allow the audience to see the puppets with a 'double-vision' – both as a 'manipulated objects' and as characters who are 'alive' – affects the audience? If so, in what way?

6. Do you think one of the advantages of making puppet theatre rather than theatre, is that the artist has control over every aspect of the production?

    Comment on any aspects you use such as sculpting, modelling, embroidery, lighting, carpentry, acting, writing, producing, designing, inventing etc., and their combination.

7. Do you want your puppets to imitate life, or to suggest a stylization or abstraction of life?

    Please comment.

    Do you use puppet theatre to flaunt social conventions – to satirize, for parody, to caricature or exaggerate, or for fantasy, or poetry?

    Please comment.

8. Puppets, performing objects and actors:

    (a) Would you define a puppet as a 'performing object'?

        If so, in which particular way? For example, are your puppets:

            Objects of narration?

            Objects of mask and costume?

            Objects of staging (like props or scenery)?

            Present as 'real' objects?

(b) Acting:

    (1) Do you use naturalism? If so, why?

    (2) Do you break the mimetic illusion so the audience does not identify with the actor (e.g. as in Kabuki)? If so, why?

    (3) Do you use mask acting so the actor is seen to have real life while the mask is an object under his control? If so, why?

9. Puppet sign-systems (or elements):

(a) Movement:

Do you think that the movement of the puppet is its most important aspect? If so, why?

Do you think it is important that a puppet moves and 'speaks' together, and that any other puppet on stage must be still while this takes place? If so, why?

(b) Design:

    (1) Design of the puppet:

Please comment on your approach to designing your puppets:

Do you allow the puppet 'character' to be represented by objects, or by metaphor or exaggeration, or use of the grotesque?

    (2) Size of the puppet:

Do you contrast puppet size with human size?

Do you contrast puppet size with size of stage/scenery/props/other puppets? To what purpose?

    (3) Visual/tactile qualities and costumes:

How, and for what purpose, do you use these in your designs?

    (4) Onstage absence/presence of operator:

Do you conceal the way puppets are controlled, for a purpose? Does this affect your overall design purpose? (e.g. in Bunraku, the life-like puppets contrast with the unlifelike presence of their operators so the audience's perception of them changes.)

Do you combine all of these to attain different levels of response in the audience?

(c) Speech:

    (1) Do you use speech and/or sound as an element in your puppet theatre?

    (2) Do you regard it necessary to simplify or scale down the system of speech you use for your puppets. If so, why?

    (3) 'The separation of the speaking subject and the physical source of the word is the distinctive feature of the puppet theatre.' (Jurkowsky)

Please comment.

(4) 'The actor's emotions and voice must coincide with the pup-pet's.' Do you agree? If so, why?

(5) Do you stylize or ritualize your puppet's speech/voice? If so, how and why?

(Do you wish to take away the difference between the figure of the puppet and the voice of the person speaking for it?)

(6) 'The onstage speaker and puppet must interact.' Do you agree?

10. Maeterlinck was interested in the 'remote and automaton-like nature of the marionette, as it fruitlessly confronts the force of destiny. Both (the puppet and man) are manipulated by outer forces, both are unaware of this control over them.'

Please comment.

Contemporary Theatre Review
1999, Vol. 10, Part 1, pp. 89–94
Reprints available directly from the publisher
Photocopying permitted by license only

Appendix B:
Puppet Theatre – the European Repertoire

Marion Baraitser

The editor is indebted to Henryk Jurkowski's detailed survey of the history of puppet theatre texts, *Ecrivains et Marionettes* (1991), as yet untranslated into English, and Harold B. Segels's recent survey *Pinocchio's Progeny* (1995), which covers the modernist period particularly well.

The impact of the puppet on literary and theatrical imagination exists far back in time. The reasons for writing puppet theatre texts are many: in the Baroque period, because it was considered equal to theatre; in eighteenth century France, to oppose the monopoly of theatre; in Germany in the first part of the nineteenth century, to stimulate a new awareness of acting; at the end of the nineteenth century, to counteract naturalism – and in our age, to rediscover and rework ancient traditions like Bunraku (Jurkowski, 1991).

For knowledge of early puppet theatre texts, we rely on descriptions of puppet theatre performances in fiction or drama. The earliest fictional reference to this is in Xenophon (430–357 AD), who refers to his symposium as a mime troupe in which puppets represented erotic characters in literature. Later Cervantes, in *Don Quixote*, describes Quixote's encounter with puppet theatre (Segal, 1995).

We know that puppet theatre moved from pantomime through narration to drama. No puppet play-texts survived from the seventeenth and eighteenth centuries. Eighteenth century texts were only transcribed and published in the nineteenth century, though their roots lay in the oral traditions of the Middle Ages. In the Middle Ages we know of travelling showmen or 'comediens' using masks and puppets at fairs. They improvised short plays based on Christian texts, legends, stories, ballads and parables, derived from medieval Italian farce written in hexameters, or from gypsy songs performed from carts in the spirit of the 'zany' or clown. They later used other oral traditions like commentaries and narratives, both political and religious. Only when these improvisations needed to be repeated, were the texts 'fixed' i.e. written down.

Actual dramatic texts for puppets only appeared in the seventeenth century and these were mostly borrowed (often from memory) from the stage. Italian troupes used opera and commedia dell'arte texts in which they alternated puppets and actors in adaptations or versions of the mysteries, melodramas and chivalric pieces. In France in 1670, the Comédie-Française held the monopoly on the performance of dialogue, so the fairground performers spoke monologues or sang dialogues, ragging the 'official' theatre the while, using commedia dell'arte characters like Polchinelle. (It was these Italian and French puppet theatre travellers who brought the malevolent Pulchinella to England, who evolved from a string-puppet into the glove-puppet with which we are familiar.) Later, French performers favoured melodramas that combined sentimentality with sensationalism, mostly aiming for exact miniatures of characters in 'real' theatre.

Apart from the puppet-text incorporated by Ben Jonson in *Bartholomew Fair*, a play-within-a-play to ridicule the Puritan authorities for banning theatre, which used voice distortion and the voice coming from 'outside' the puppet to avoid censorship, the first works deliberately written for puppet theatre in the second half of the seventeenth century were mostly opera texts written by poets or writers working on the theatre 'fringe.' These were presented by artists who were not actually puppeteers.

The fascination with puppets, both literary and dramatic grew in the eighteenth century. The Englishmen Samuel Foote, granted a licence to manage the Haymarket Theatre, London, in the eighteenth century, having survived the draconian Licensing Act of 1737 and the loss of a leg in a riding accident, used his considerable talent as an actor–director to satirise English follies of the day (including a satire on his own wooden leg, which he felt gave him equality with the wooden puppets in his shows.) By including puppet plays in his repertoire, Foote discovered the effectiveness of separating the characters' 'voice' and 'image', and in so doing, anticipated the ideas of Kleist and Gordon Craig of substituting puppets for actors.

In the late eighteenth century in Germany, as part of the 'Sturm-und-Drang' Romantic movement, the metaphor for man as a passive 'puppet' in the hands of a Destiny that controlled him, surfaced in Goethe's early 'Puppenspiel' (not written for performance) and in the references to puppets in *Wilhelm Meister's Apprenticeship*. But it was the great German dramatist Heinrich Kleist's essay, 'On the Puppet Theatre', that had a far-reaching effect on theatre. Kleist wanted to show how a 'low' or popular art form like children's puppet theatre, that uses folk language and that rediscovers the 'unconscious' and the intuitive, can reanimate 'high' art.

Kleist thought that, because the puppet lacks consciousness, the puppet's actions and gestures hold more 'grace' and spontaneity than the 'dancer/actor'.

Maurice Sand began his celebrated puppet theatre 'The Theatre of Friends' in the 1840's as glove-puppet performances to cheer up his mother, George Sand – who had experimented with theatre at Nohant. It resulted in the publication of a collection of his puppet theatre texts, 'Le Theatre des Marionettes'. (Napoleon 111's censorship law demanded that theatre texts be in published form so they could be scrutinised.) This resulted, later, in a joint study of commedia dell'arte done with his mother. Maurice Sand regarded his finger puppets (for which he sculpted heads) as 'alive', because they express the 'I' of the manipulator.

With the rise of modernism at the turn of the century and the reaction against scientism, realism and bourgeois values, there was a surge of renewed interest in the puppet theatre as an area of creativity to be taken seriously by artists. Schopenhauer's idea that 'the world is my representation (of it)' – that art does not represent reality, but is separate from it – spilled over into the new metaphor of man as the puppeteer, the little god who rules his own world.

The Belgian playwright Maurice Maeterlinck, whose aesthetics of symbolic theatre incorporated in his essay 'The Tragedy of the Everyday', used 'death, dreams, instincts, hypnosis, magnetism and psychic forces' to draw the audience into the mysteries of the spiritual and eternal human soul. Not surprisingly, for this purpose he needed a 'new actor' – Maeterlinck thought that the human being could be replaced by 'a shadow, a reflection, projections' or even wax figures, to match his vision of man as blind, as unconscious, as full of chance as the 'Death' that faces him. Maeterlinck wrote an early trilogy of puppet plays, published in 1894 (though perhaps he envisaged them played by puppet-like actors), and incorporated puppets into his other incantatory musical and atmospheric structures.

Puppet theatre was also incorporated into artistic cabaret across Europe at the turn of the century – the 'Chat Noir' in Paris famous for its 'Chinese shadows'; the 'Four Cats' (Quatre Gats') in Barcelona for Catalan artists, in which Picasso participated; 'Eleven Executioners' in Munich, famous for Willi Rath's anti-imperialist *The Fine Family*, set in the Boer War; Vienna's 'Bat' puppet theatre which staged Oscar Kokoschka's 'comedy for automatons'; '*Sphinx and Strawman* showing man as a sexual puppet, and Cracow's 'Green Balloon' where Wyspianski took the indigenous 'szopka' (from 'booth'), or nativity puppet play, and adapted it to political cabaret.

Alfred Jarry laid the foundations of his puppet play *Ubu Roi* at school, to lampoon his physics teacher, Monsieur Ebé (hence Ubu), which he set in Poland (a never-never land that had disappeared off the map at the time). It was first performed as a play for puppets at his make-shift 'Theatre des Phynances', at home in 1888, and performed again for fellow students in a tiny theatre in Paris. *Ubu Roi* surfaced in 1896, when Jarry had become a writer (*Ubu Roi* had already been published), and a manager of Lugne-Poe's experimental Theatre de l'Oeuvre in Paris. He was left to mount the show himself, which he decided to project as a grand 'guignol' or Punch and Judy show. For strong alienation effects, he used live actors in masks who moved jerkily like marionettes, using voice distortion. The backdrop was a crudely painted from a child's viewpoint, and an old man hung notices at the side of the stage signifying scene changes. Jarry wanted the text to shock and offend the French bourgeoisie, so he wrote his version of a bawdy, grotesque send-up of Shakespeare's 'Macbeth' that provoked the audience by its violence and grotesquerie. The play changed the face of theatre and Paris erupted, provoking riots, ridicule and debate.

The Flemish dramatist Michel de Ghelderode, took music hall and the ancient Flemish marionette theatre that he loved all his life, as the models for his own works, which stand half-way between Jarry and Artaud, in which man is seen as a plaything of the gods. 'Marionettes, because of their natural reserve and perfect silence, manage to console me for the cacophony of the play and the crazy glibness of the impudent creatures that theatre people most often are. I owe them the revelation of the theatre, the theatre in its pure state, the theatre in its savage state, the original theatre.' (Iglasias & Trutor, 1956).

Modernist Spanish writers used puppet theatre to debunk traditionalism and stultifying literary models. Ramón de Valle-Inclán invented a grotesque parodic drama he called 'esperpento' (from the word for 'distorting mirror'), some of which were censored, and extensively used puppets and marionettes in his plays to mask his underlying contempt for anything that needed debunking (especially the monarchy and the military). From his early puppet play, *The Dragon's Head* (ostensibly a fairy-tale but in reality satirising the Spanish court), to his 'Puppet Theatre of Avarice, Love and Death' (1927), he wrote puppet plays in which, like a puppeteer, he could stand outside and view the world as small, ridiculous and absurd. Inclán's successor was Lorca, whose upbringing among the peasants of Andalusia inspired him to put on puppet shows at home in Grenada (with Manuel de Falla at the piano). His early interest in folklore led him to write and stage his early puppet play *The Billy-Club Puppets: Tragicomedy of Don Cristobal and Miss Rosita* – a robust puppet farce full of slapstick. In a shorter version, Lorca's prologue and the Director's closing address, focus on the primitive vitality of puppet theatre and its folk origins, and establishes that it is this force, which will drive away the tedium and vulgarity of Spanish theatre: 'The poet who has interpreted and adapted this puppet farce from the lips of the people has evidence of the fact that the distinguished audience this afternoon will be able to appreciate, with intelligence and good heart, the delicious and crude language of the puppets.'

Schnitzler's *The Great Pater Puppet Theatre*, in its unprinted form, was staged by the first German cabaret and parodied 'amusement park' puppetry, using actors and puppets together. In a play-within-a-play, Schnitzler not only places on stage the carping bourgeois audience who criticise Schnitzler's own plays for being too full of sex, but also the Director, who quarrels with the Author. Schnitzler makes the point that man has less humanity than a puppet. There is a mysterious and terrifying character, the Unknown One, who decides who is 'human' and who is a 'puppet', who 'manipulates' and who does not, then cuts all the strings of the marionettes, puts out all the stage lights, brings down the Director and then disappears, allowing 'normality' to reign on stage once more.

The early twentieth century avant-garde makers of theatre used puppet theatre to express their view of man as a machine. Marinetti, the founder of Italian Futurism, wrote *Electric Puppets (Sexual Electricity* in its later abbreviated form) at the same time as his manifesto celebrating machine technology. The play caused a storm, as it showed 'live' actors personifying a married couple who enliven their marriage by kissing behind the backs of mechanical puppets that they use as voyeurs to their love-making. By this scenario, Marinetti satirised the bourgeois audience who needed his 'Holy electricity' to waken them from their own deadly boredom. On the other hand, Karel Kapek wrote puppet plays as a form of Expressionism, portraying his horror at the idea of machines dominating humans. The theatre of the Bauhaus used live actors as stylized geometric shapes resembling puppets and automatons in dance and pantomimes that were also part of the 'machine-culture'.

The interest in puppets continued well into the 1930's. As late as 1949, George Bernard Shaw wrote a puppet play, *Shakes versus Shaw* expressing the mystery of the phenomenon of the puppet. He was sent puppet figures of himself and Shakespeare by an English puppeteer, who asked Shaw to write a ten-minute piece about them. Shaw writes in his preface to the play, of the puppet's 'unvarying intensity of facial expression, impossible for living actors, (that) keeps the imagination of the spectator continuously stimulated.' (Shaw 1949)

Post World War II writers brought a new perspective to the puppet figure. American writers like Jean-Claude van Itallie used larger-than-life dolls to satirize the violence in ordinary American life. Brecht's successor in East Germany, Heiner Müller used puppets dolls and robots to show up the grotesquerie of Prussian repression. By the 1970's Tadeusz Kantor, the celebrated Polish theatre director who founded Cricot 2 with Maria Jarema, toured his famous productions of *The Dead Class* and *Wiepole/ Wiepole*, which reflected his interest in puppetry to express his view of death and destruction brought about by two world wars. He founded a puppet theatre at the Academy of Fine Arts in Cracow in 1938, where he mounted Maeterlinck's *Death of Tintagiles* as an experiment in combining Symbolism with his own avant-garde ideas. He went on to develop his concept of 'mannequins' in his own work, through experimentation with the staging of Witkiewitcz's plays. In his essay 'The Theatre of Death', Kantor disputes Gordon Craig's ideas that the human actor could be displaced by puppet-actors and adds a new connection between the 'mannequin' and death: 'Mannequins also have their own version of Transgressions. The existence of these creatures, shaped in man's image, almost 'godlessly', in an illegal fashion, is the result of heretical dealings, a manifestation of the Dark, Nocturnal, Rebellious side of human activity. Of Crimes and Traces of Death as sources of recognition.... from this entity, so similar to a living human being, but deprived of consciousness and purpose, there is transmitted to us a terrifying message of Death and Nothingness... imitation and deceptive similarity, which serve the conjurer... The Mannequin in my theatre must become a Model through which passes a strong sense of Death and the condition of the Dead. A model for the Live Actor (14. Kobkalka (1993)). In his plays, Kantor uses mannequins, dummies and wax figures as doubles of the living selves of the dead that he represents on stage. His plays pointed the way for the present postmodern period.

Contemporary Theatre Review
1999, Vol. 10, Part 1, p. 95
Reprints available directly from the publisher
Photocopying permitted by license only

Select Bibliography

Allen & Shaw. (1992) Editors. *On the Brink of Belonging*. p. 15. London. Calouste Gulbenkian Foundation.

Iglusias & Trutor. (1956) Editors. 'Les Entretiens d'Ostende'.

Jurkowski, H. (1979) Literary Views on Puppet theatre. In *Aspects of Puppet Theatre* (1988) edited by P. Francis. pp. 1–32. London: Puppet Centre Trust.

Jurkowski, H. (1991) 'Ecrivains et Marionettes: Quatres siècles de litterature dramatique en Europe'. pp. 58–64. Editions Institute International de la Marionette. Charleville-Mezieres.

Kobialka, M. (1993). 'A Journey through Other Places: Essays and other Manifestos, 1994–1990'. Editor and Translator.

Obratsov, S. (1957) 'My Profession'. Moscow. Foreign Language Publication House.

Shaw, B. (1962) 'Complete Plays with Prefaces'. Vol. 15. New York. Dodd, Mead & Co.

Segel, H. (1995) *'Pinocchio's Progeny'*. PAJ Books. John Hopkins University Press. Baltimore and London.

Sherger, D. & J. (1987) Editors. *Humor and Comedy in Puppetry*. p. 1. Ohio. Bowling Green State University.

Speaight, G. (1990) pp. 183–190. 'The History of the English Puppet Theatre'. Robert Hale.

Tillis. (1992) *Towards an Aesthetic of the Puppet*. p. 6. USA. Greenwood Press.

Contemporary Theatre Review
1999, Vol. 10, Part 1, pp. 97–98
Reprints available directly from the publisher
Photocopying permitted by license only

Notes on Contributors

Marion Baraitser taught literature for London University's Extramural Department before becoming an Arts Council and BBC commissioned playwright and short story writer. She is currently working on an adaptation of 'The Story of an African Farm' with the Royal National Theatre Studio, which will be broadcast on BBC Radio 4 June 1996, and a novel about London. After *Women in Publishing* shortlisted her as editor of '*Plays by Mediterranean Women*', she started her own press, *Loki Books* co-publishing with UNESCO.

DOO COT was formed in 1990 when Nenagh Watson and Rachael Field joined forces as painter and puppeteer. Inspired by the urbanisation of Manchester, together with musician Sylvia Hallett, they created performances that linked puppetry, visual art and live music for adult audiences. *Odd If you Dare* was selected for the Barclay's New Play Festival, 1995.

Rachael Field and Nenagh Watson live together in 'The Hidden Museum', Whalley Range, Manchester with their five hamsters and a rabbit.

Johanna Enckell studied in Helsinki, Paris and New Orleans before teaching at Oulu and Helsinki universities, and becoming deputy director of the Finnish Theatre Academy of Helsinki. Today, she is a freelance playwright, director and theatre critic and divides her time between Finland and France. In 1996, two of her latest productions were mounted in Paris: *Orlando* (using animated objects and puppets), and *Who Killed van Gogh* (an adaptation of Antonin Artaud's text). The combination of acting and animation is a hallmark of her texts and direction. In 1990 she won the annual Finnish drama award, the Lea prize for her plays *Saint Bridget's Dangerous Games* and *A Woman of a Hundred Dreams*.

Eric Bass has worked in the theatre since 1970 as a director, performer, writer, mask maker and puppet maker. He began as a street performer in New York City and, in 1975, joined Jean Erdman's 'Theatre of the Open

Eye,' a total theatre company combining elements of dance, acting and music in original pieces based on myth. The company was strongly influenced by Ms Erdman's husband, the eminent mythologist, Joseph Campbell. In 1980, Mr Bass left 'Theatre of the Open eye' to create his first solo piece using puppets, *Autumn Portraits* which won international awards at festivals in Australia, Hungary and the USA. In 1982, Mr Bass moved to Munich, Germany to co-found a company, Sandglass Theatre, together with his wife-to-be, Ines Zeller. Nearly all the Sandglass Theatre productions explore the human actor's relationship with the puppet. Sandglass productions have toured worldwide in Europe, Australia, Japan, Israel and the USA. Since 1986, the company has been based in Putney, Vermont, where it now also plays in its own barn theatre.

In addition to creating works for Sandglass Theatre, Eric Bass has directed works by Shakespeare, Brecht, Anski and contemporary playwrights in theatres in Finland, Switzerland, Poland, Canada and the USA. All of these productions have experimented with the relationship between the actor and the puppet as a theatrical medium. Mr Bass has published one play, *In My Grandmother's Purse*, a play for children, which has been produced in three countries. Eric Bass has taught workshops in his art, most frequently at the Stuttgart Hochschule fur Darstellende Kunst, and is currently a Guest Professor of Theatre at Marlboro College, Vermont. In 1991, Mr Bass was awarded the prestigious Figurentheater Prize for the city of Erlangen, Germany, for his collected work.

Dennis Silk has performed his Thing Theatre plays in Israel, in English or in Hebrew, solo or with others, over the past 25 years. He has worked in particular with Fa chu, a Chinese choreographer who has directed five of his plays.

He hopes for a combination of 'live' actors, puppets, toys, dolls and things, and a 'thingification' of language itself, and of stage space.

CONTEMPORARY THEATRE REVIEW
AN INTERNATIONAL JOURNAL

Notes for contributors

Submission of a paper will be taken to imply that it represents original work not previously published, that it is not being considered for publication elsewhere and that, if accepted for publication, it will not be published elsewhere in the same form, in any language, without the consent of editor and publisher. It is a condition of acceptance by the editor of a typescript for publication that the publisher automatically acquires the copyright of the typescript throughout the world. It will also be assumed that the author has obtained all necessary permissions to include in the paper items such as quotations, musical examples, figures, tables etc. Permissions should be paid for prior to submission.

Typescripts. Papers should be submitted in triplicate to the Editors, *Contemporary Theatre Review*, c/o Harwood Academic Publishers, at:

5th Floor, Reading Bridge House		820 Town Center Drive		3-14-9, Okubo
Reading Bridge Approach	or	Langhorne	or	Shinjuku-ku
Reading RGl 8PP		PA 19047 USA		Tokyo 169
UK				Japan

Papers should be typed or word processed with double spacing on one side of good quality ISO A4 (212 × 297 mm) paper with a 3 cm left-hand margin. Papers are accepted only in English.

Abstracts and Keywords. Each paper requires an abstract of 100–150 words summarizing the significant coverage and findings, presented on a separate sheet of paper. Abstracts should be followed by up to six key words or phrases which, between them, should indicate the subject matter of the paper. These will be used for indexing and data retrieval purposes.

Figures. All figures (photographs, schema, charts, diagrams and graphs) should be numbered with consecutive arabic numerals, have descriptive captions and be mentioned in the text. Figures should be kept separate from the text but an approximate position for each should be indicated in the margin of the typescript. It is the author's responsibility to obtain permission for any reproduction from other sources.

Preparation: Line drawings must be of a high enough standard for direct reproduction; photocopies are not acceptable. They should be prepared in black (india) ink on white art paper, card or tracing paper, with all the lettering and symbols included. Computer-generated graphics of a similar high quality are also acceptable, as are good sharp photoprints ("glossies"). Computer print-outs must be completely legible. Photographs intended for halftone reproduction must be good glossy original prints of maximum contrast. Redrawing or retouching of unusable figures will be charged to authors.

Size: Figures should be planned so that they reduce to 12 cm column width. The preferred width of line drawings is 24 cm, with capital lettering 4 mm high, for reduction by one-half. Photographs for halftone reproduction should be approximately twice the desired finished size.

Captions: A list of figure captions, with the relevant figure numbers, should be typed on a separate sheet of paper and included with the typescript.

Musical examples: Musical examples should be designated as "Figure 1" etc., and the recommendations above for preparation and sizing should be followed. Examples must be well prepared and of a high standard for reproduction, as they will not be redrawn or retouched by the printer.

In the case of large scores, musical examples will have to be reduced in size and so some clarity will be lost. This should be borne in mind especially with orchestral scores.

Notes are indicated by superior arabic numerals without parentheses. The text of the notes should be collected at the end of the paper.

References are indicated in the text by the name and date system either "Recent work (Smith & Jones, 1987, Robinson, 1985, 1987) . . ." or "Recently Smith & Jones (1987) . . ." If a publication has more than three authors, list all names on the first occurrence; on subsequent occurrences use the first author's name plus "*et al.*" Use an ampersand rather than "and" between the last two authors. If there is more than one publication by the same author(s) in the same year, distinguish by adding a, b, c etc. to both the text citation and the list of references (e.g. "Smith, 1986a") References should be collected and typed in alphabetical order after the Notes and Acknowledgements sections (if these exist). Examples:

Benedetti, J. (1988) *Stanislavski*, London: Methuen

Granville-Barker, H. (1934) Shakespeare's dramatic art. In *A Companion to Shakespeare Studies*, edited by H. Granville-Barker and G. B. Harrison, p. 84. Cambridge: Cambridge University Press

Johnston, D. (1970) Policy in theatre. *Hibernia*, **16**, 16

Proofs. Authors will receive page proofs (including figures) by air mail for correction and these must be returned as instructed within 48 hours of receipt. Please ensure that a full postal address is given on the first page of the typescript so that proofs are not delayed in the post. Authors' alterations, other than those of a typographical nature, in excess of 10% of the original composition cost, will be charged to authors.

Page Charges. There are no page charges to individuals or institutions.

INSTRUCTIONS FOR AUTHORS

ARTICLE SUBMISSION ON DISK

The Publisher welcomes submissions on disk. The instructions that follow are intended for use by authors whose articles have been accepted for publication and are in final form. Your adherence to these guidelines will facilitate the processing of your disk by the typesetter. These instructions do not replace the journal Notes for Contributors; all information in Notes for Contributors remains in effect.

When typing your article, do not include design or formatting information. Type all text flush left, unjustified and without hyphenation. Do not use indents, tabs or multi-spacing. If an indent is required, please note it by a line space; also mark the position of the indent on the hard copy manuscript. Indicate the beginning of a new paragraph by typing a line space. Leave one space at the end of a sentence, after a comma or other punctuation mark, and before an opening parenthesis. Be sure not to confuse lower case letter "l" with numeral "1", or capital letter "O" with numeral "0". Distinguish opening quotes from close quotes. Do not use automatic page numbering or running heads.

Tables and displayed equations may have to be rekeyed by the typesetter from your hard copy manuscript. Refer to the journal Notes for Contributors for style for Greek characters, variables, vectors, etc.

Articles prepared on most word processors are acceptable. If you have imported equations and/or scientific symbols into your article from another program, please provide details of the program used and the procedures you followed. If you have used macros that you have created, please include them as well.

You may supply illustrations that are available in an electronic format on a separate disk. Please clearly indicate on the disk the file format and/or program used to produce them, and supply a high-quality hard copy of each illustration. Submit your disk when you submit your final hard copy manuscript. The disk file and hard copy must match exactly.

If you are submitting more than one disk, please number each disk. Please mark each disk with the journal title, author name, abbreviated article title and file names.

Be sure to retain a back-up copy of each disk submitted. Pack your disk carefully to avoid damage in shipping, and submit it with your hard copy manuscript and complete Disk Specifications form (see reverse) to the person designated in the journal Notes for Contributors.

GORDON AND BREACH PUBLISHERS • **HARWOOD ACADEMIC PUBLISHERS**

Disk Specifications

Journal name _____

_____

Date _____ **Paper Reference Number** _____

Paper title _____

_____

_____

Corresponding author _____

Address _____

_____

_____

_____ **Postcode** _____

Telephone _____

Fax _____

E-mail _____

Disks Enclosed (file names and descriptions of contents)

Text

Disk 1 _____

Disk 2 _____

Disk 3 _____

PLEASE RETAIN A BACK-UP COPY OF ALL DISK FILES SUBMITTED.

GORDON AND BREACH PUBLISHERS • **HARWOOD ACADEMIC PUBLISHERS**

Figures

Disk 1 _____

Disk 2 _____

Disk 3 _____

Computer make and model _____

_____

Size/format of floppy disks

☐ 3.5"   ☐ 5.25"

☐ Single sided   ☐ Double sided

☐ Single density ☐ Double density   ☐ High density

Operating system _____

Version _____

Word processor program _____

Version _____

Imported maths/science program _____

Version _____

Graphics program _____

Version _____

Files have been saved in the following format

Text: _____

Figures: _____

Maths: _____

PLEASE RETAIN A BACK-UP COPY OF ALL DISK FILES SUBMITTED.

GORDON AND BREACH PUBLISHERS   •   **HARWOOD ACADEMIC PUBLISHERS**